THE APOCATASTASIS;

OR

PROGRESS BACKWARDS.

A NEW "TRACT FOR THE TIMES."

BY THE AUTHOR.

Παν δε το κινουμενον, και χρονου μετεχον, αιδιον ον, χρηται περιοδοις, και περιοδικως ανακυκλειται και αποκαθιϛαται απο των αυτων επι τα αυτα δηλονοτι.   Proclus, Institut. Theol. C. cxcviii.

TRANSLATION.—Whatever, having a permanent being, (folly for instance,) nevertheless partakes of the vicissitudes of time, and is moveable, useth periods is circularly moved, and manifestly, hath its Apocatastasis from the same to the same.

BURLINGTON:
CHAUNCEY GOODRICH.
1854.

Entered according to act of Congress, by
CHAUNCEY GOODRICH,
In the Clerk's Office in the District of Vermont in the year 1854.

CHAPTER I.

Fata quoque, et vitas hominum suspendit ab astris.
Manilii Astronomicon, iii. 58.

Αςερες ουρανιοι, Νυκτος φιλα τεκνα μελαινης,
εγκυκλιοις δινησι περιθρονιοι κυκλεοντες,
ανταυγεις, πυροεντες, αει γενετηρες απαντων·
μοιριδιοι, πασης μοιρης σημαντορες οντες·
θνητων ανθρωπων θειην διεποντες αταρπον:
ελθετ',   Orphica H. vii. 3–7.

Ye stars celestial! Children of black Night,
Wheeling, enthroned sublime, in circling Orbs,
Effulgent, genitors of all events,
Who Fate obey, and who all fates dispose,
Their lot appointing unto mortal men,
All hail!

"The sun ariseth, and the sun goeth down, and hasteth to his place where he arose. The wind goeth toward the south and turneth about unto the north, it whirleth about continually; and the wind returneth again according to his circuits. All the rivers run into the sea, yet the sea is not full; unto the place from whence the rivers came, thither they return again.

The thing that hath been, it is that which shall be; and that which is done is that which shall be done; and there is no new thing under the sun. Is there anything whereof it may be said, See, this is new? it hath been already of old time, which was before us." (Solomon.)

The Preacher, doubtless, speaks truth here, yet he speaks somewhat superficially, or as a mere outside observer. He does not unveil the causes, and announce to us the Law in obedience to which all terrestrial things not only "flow" but revolve, evermore moving onward, and onward, without let or stay, yet evermore returning, and coming round, full circle, to the points through which, before, many times, it may be, they have already passed. Perhaps he had not investigated the subject,—being of pretty extensive business engagements—and having, besides, much other literary work on hand: or perhaps the mere "weariness to the flesh," induced by "much study," which extorted "vanity of vanities! all is vanity!" "of making books there is no end," may have made him content to assert the bare fact, of the incessant and stale iteration of things, while he was not in the mood to go into explanations, which, nevertheless, he may have been very competent to give. His silence, however, from whatever cause it may have originated, is the less to be regretted, because other wise men have spoken fully to the point which Solomon overlooked or neglected.

"The blessed body which revolves in a circle, (the visible heavens,) is the cause of the events in the sublunary world. For both are parts of the universe, and they have a certain relation to each other. If, therefore, the cause of generation in the things which surround us, originates in the natures which are above us, it follows that the seeds of things which happen here, descend from thence. And if some one should add, since astronomy gives credibility to this, that there are *apocatastatic* periods of the stars and spheres, some of which are simple but others compounded, such a one will partly accord with the Egyptians, and partly with the Grecians. A man of this kind, therefore, will not deny that in consequence of the same motions returning, effects also will return together with their causes ; and that lives on the earth, generations, educations, dispositions and fortunes, will be the same with those that formerly existed." (Synesius de Providentia.)— These apocatastatic periods (περιοδοι, completed revolutions,) of the stars or spheres are of several kinds, as intimated in the above extract, and of course come round at different intervals. Two of the heavenly bodies may come to have the same relative position to each other which they had at some preceding time; as when the earth, at any given point of its orbit, has the same relation to the sun which it had a year before;—or the earth, sun, and moon ; or these with one, or with more than one, of the planets, may come to the same relative position which they have been in before, and this, happening at different intervals for each combination of bodies, will be, for each combination, their apocatastatic period. Or the entire number of astronomical bodies may come to the same relative position they have had before. "The end therefore of the mundane year is, when all the planets and all the fixed stars have returned from a certain place to the same place, so that no star in the heavens may be situated in a place different from that in which it was before. * * * * * * This, however, according to the decision of physiologists, will take place at the expiration of 15,000 years. * * * * This year, therefore, is called the truly revolving year" &c. (Macrobius, in Somn. Scip. lib. ii.)

According to Firmicius, (Mathesis lib. iii) this is called the greater apocatastasis, and consists of 300,000 years. If then we suppose this period to commence from the present position of the heavens, all events on the earth for the next 300,000 years, or 15,000 years, the difference is not much, will be identically the same that they have been for the last 300,000, or 15,000 years. The successive apocatastatic periods of smaller numbers of heavenly bodies, instead of producing the same, will produce similar sublunary events, and these will be like in proportion to the number and sameness of siderial powers which combine to produce them. So much, and it would seem

to be sufficient, as of unquestionable authority, we may rely upon, without the aid of Solomon, in explanation of his assertion of the perpeutual reiteration of things under the sun. But not only are these periods different in duration, but they are different in the character and quality of the terrestrial effects they produce ; the periods of different stars or combinations of stars, bringing about different results,—those of the same, the same, or similar results. "Not only with respect to terrestrial plants, but likewise in terrestrial animals, a fertility and sterility of soul as well as of body takes place, when the revolutions of the heavenly bodies complete the periphery of their respective orbits ; which are shorter to the shorter lived, and contrarywise to such as are the contrary." (Plato, de Republica, viii.) That is, the apocatastatic periods of some stars are shorter, and of others longer ; those of some are periods of sterility and degeneracy of men, animals, and plants ; those of others, periods of fertility and excellence. Thus, though the great cycle of 300,000 years is constantly repeating itself with all its same sublunary events, this does not prevent that it may include within itself many smaller revolutions which repeat themselves, with their similar terrestrial results, at various intervals ; in fact it consists of these shorter circumvolutions : " With centric and eccentric scribbled o'er,
                    Cycle and epicycle, orb in orb."
witness, as the celestial orbs revolve, and come to their various apocatastatic positions, the constant repetition of night and day ; the return of similar seasons ; the emergence from barbarism, the culmination, and the decay, of nations—return to the same point of barbarism from whence they started ; and this process repeating itself perpetually in the same nations, the several mutations exhibiting essentially the same phases at each successive revolution. Yet these historico-dramatic exhibitions of terrestrial events will be the same with a difference,—the players are different, or if they are the same (Plato, de Repub. Lib. X) they are, unfortunately, not permitted to remember how they played before ; and then in every large but partial cycle there may be some adjacent body which holds a different

relation to it at different revolutions; or some interloping comet may cross the orbit of the period, modifying or dislocating its history at some points. We are not, therefore, to understand Solomon quite literally. We are not to expect, in comparing one partial apocatastatic period with another, or rather, the same period with itself in its successive revolutions, to find, in earthly relations, an exact parallel and identity. It is sufficient if we recognize a strong family likeness, a characteristic resemblance in most things, although there may be decided otherness in others, owing to temporary, accidental disturbing influences. Or single traits of the most decided similarity may characterize two successive periods, traits which may be quite accidental, and foreign to their true physiognomy and which may disappear in the third; as where the tails of two different but equal comets happen to pass severally across the same portion of their orbit during the two contiguous revolutions. In order to ascertain, in regard to two historical periods which remind us of one another, whether they are really apocatastatic, it is not always necessary to consult the astronomers, or the astrological doctors, to know whether their beginnings coincide chronologically with the apocatastatic position, and as it were, meeting in conclave, of the same celestial notabilities; it will be sufficient to determine by inspection whether they both belong to Plato's periods, either of fertility or of sterility, that is, whether they are both fertile or both barren periods in the Platonic sense. And by way of example and specimen of such periods, and of the proper method of detecting them, I will make a quotation from a most learned and very extraordinary man, one peculiarly well qualified to have an opinion in such abstruse matters, a sort of christian heathen, in the midst of Christendom in the nineteenth century, a man who honestly and manfully went over from Jehovah to Jupiter, a Julian on a small scale. Listen to his profession of faith in a Note on the following passage in his translation of Marinus' Life of Proclus. "But he purified himself every month, by the sacred rites in honour of the mother of the gods, celebrated by the Romans, and prior to them by the Phrygians: he likewise more diligently observed the unfortunate days of the Egyptians, than they themselves; and besides this, fasted on certain days in a peculiar manner on account of the lunar appearances." So far from the Life;—the Note is as follows: " A genuine modern will doubtless consider the whole of Proclus' religious conduct as ridiculously superstitious. And so, indeed, at first sight, it appears; but he who has penetrated the depths of ancient wisdom, will find in it more than meets the vulgar ear. The religion of the Heathens, has indeed, for many centuries, been the object of ridicule and contempt; yet the author of the present work is not ashamed to own, *that he is a perfect convert to it in every particular*, so far as it was understood and illustrated by the Pythagoric and Platonic Philosophers." I have called the author of the above an extraordinary man, not because a christian heathen is anything extraordinary at the present time, they are thick as autumn leaves, but because few of them have the magnanimity to renounce their baptism, and profess publicly their adhesion to the " Dii Majores et gentium." I desire, however, to take this occasion to acknowledge my obligations to the gentleman in question,—not for his heathenism but for his learning—for I shall often, in the course of this work, find it much more convenient to use his translations than to make them for myself, besides that, in many cases, the originals are not within my reach. Where I cannot avail myself of his aid I must not be expected to translate with his admirable closeness to the original; I shall however hope to give the true meaning of the passages cited, or where I am in doubt I will give the original itself. Such show of learning is not to my taste, but in the present instance, as the reader will perceive bye and bye, it appears to be unavoidable. But to the promised quotation.— "The different periods in which these mutations happen, are called by Plato, with great propriety, periods of *fertility and sterility;* for in these periods a fertility or sterility of men, irrational animals, and plants, takes place; so that in fertile periods mankind will be both more numerous, and upon the whole, superior in mental and bodily endowments, to the men of a barren period. And a similar reasoning must be extended to animals and plants. The so much celebrated heroic age was the result of one of these fertile periods, in which men, transcending the herd of mankind, both in practical and intellectual virtue, abounded on the earth. And a barren period may be considered as having commenced somewhat prior to the Augustan age, the destruction of all the great cities, with all their rites, philosophy, &c., being the natural consequence of such a period. It appears to me that this period commenced in the time of Sylla, and I found this opinion on the following passage in Plutarch's life of that great commander. "But the greatest of all (the signs prior to the civil wars) was the following: On a cloudless and clear day, the sound of a trumpet was heard, so acute, and *mournful*, as to astonish and terrify by its loudness, all that heard it. The Tuscan wise men and soothsayers, therefore, declared that this prodigy signified the mutation into, and commencement of another age.— For, according to them, there are eight ages, differing from each other in lives and manners, each of which is limited by divinity to a certain time of duration, and the number of years of which this time consists is bounded by the period of the great year. Hence when one age is finished, and another is about to commence, a certain wonderful sign will present itself, either from the earth or the heavens. The *mournfulness* of this sound of the trumpet was evidently an indication that a barren period was about to commence." (Thomas Taylor, Translation of Firmicius, Note d.)

Thus we find the weight of authority in favor of the controling influence of apocatastatic periods to be very great, and we need no longer be in doubt in regard to the reasons of the iterations of things earthly. We see too why the smaller cycles of events may repeat themselves with a difference, for only the "greater apocatastasis" can have *all* its relation identically the same. It is manifest too, that the same apocatastatic series may take place in one part of the earth in one period, and in another part of it in the next period. For, suppose the earth itself not to be one of the celestial bodies whose return to their apocatastatic position is to give character to the period in question; it follows that the earth may be in different parts of its annual orbit, and of its diurnal revolution, at the two successive apocatastatic moments or points of time, that is, for I wish to be understood, at the instant of one apocatastatic position of the stars that rule the period, the earth may be in one place, and at the next apocatastasis of the same stars, in another place. Hence, plainly, if the "seeds of things which happen here descend from thence," and the apocatastatic moment is the seed-time; the seeds which descend may, at different apocatastases, fall upon different parts of the earth's surface; so that events which before happened in one hemisphere, may have their second rehearsal in the other; or what was before in one longitude may have its next event in another. Hence, too, the same specific events, products of the same "seeds," may exhibit widely differing varieties at the different plantings; just as specifically the same tree in Italy will differ from itself in America, and that at the base of a mountain will be quite unlike itself at the top.

But whither, quoth the practical reader, does this talk tend? Do you not, then, immediately perceive, my sagacious friend, that its direction is towards the most practical results imaginable? For, if it were made known to you that on Wednesday next you were to start a journey, would you not be looking after your trunks? Or if a voyage were announced, would you not hasten to provide sea stores? Does not the husbandman, in winter, make ready for the joyous labors of spring, because he knows that the apocatastasis of the earth and sun will then open his fields for cultivation? Does not the merchant raise his wharves above the ordinary level of the Ocean, and even above that of everyday tides, because he foresees that the return of the Sun and Moon to certain former relative positions will be attended with high water? But these are small influences of one or two astronomical bodies, repeated at short intervals; how much more, then, where numbers of the celestial spheres meet in solemn conclave to determine again, and predetermine, the whole series of earthly events, it may be, for a thousand years, not only in the physical and physiological, but in the intellectual and moral regions;—how much more, could that order of events be foreknown to men as they fore know the succession of the seasons and the times of the tides, might such a knowledge be of the utmost practical value to mankind. If, then, by the aid of the genethliaci, or other mathematical and star-gazing people, or by other means, as intimated and exemplified in the quotation from Mr. Thomas Taylor, it could be certainly determined to what historic period our own, for instance, holds apocatastatic relation; what a chart were it in this uncertain sea, for the statesman, the philanthropist, the divine, and indeed for all men. How might nations provide for foreseen collisions with other nations, or guard themselves, like the prescient ruler of Egypt, against a coming scarcity;—how might the philanthropist prepare and adapt his charities to the very needs that were about to demand them;—the physician prearm himself to do battle with the pestilence which he saw in the distance;—the divine furnish himself with arguments wherewith to combat the errors, delusions, and false religions, the character of which, and the time of whose arrival he knew beforehand;—how might the fortunate man be more than doubly fortunate in the preenjoyment of his coming prosperity;—and the unfortunate strengthen himself against evils which he saw to be inevitable. How might it not be, for all men, almost as if each individual should be permitted to repeat his own life, in order to avail himself of the experience acquired in his first crude and unsatisfactory experiment, in order not to do what he had before done wrong, and to do better what little if any he might have done well;—which, who would not rejoice at the opportunity of attempting?

Do you, O, doubting reader, doubt the reality of such apocatastatic repetitions of terrestrial events? how then do you account for the solemn asseveration of Solomon? or what presumption must you be possessed of if you yield not to the authority of the "divine Plato," the "divine Plutarch," the "divine Proclus," the "divine Iamblichus," and the Divine, Synesius, who was besides a bishop.

Or do you profanely answer me that if all events on earth are thus planted and predetermined by the celestial conclaves, the "conscia fati sidera," that human foreknowledge cannot avail to alter or avoid what is preordained to be? my unthinking friend, you are like a non-orthodox sinner caviling at the foreknowledge of God, which as any old theologian can inform you, is one of the most pregnant signs of reprobation.

CHAPTER II.

*Look here, upon this picture, and on this;
The counterfeit presentment of two brothers.*
                                        HAMLET.

Inasmuch, therefore, as it has now been sufficiently demonstrated, to all men capable of appreciating an argument, that all mundane, and especially all sublunary, and terrestrial, affairs recur, come back, and copy themselves apocatastatically, as the tides follow the moon incessantly round the earth; and since it must be obvious to all properly disciplined, and truly thoughtful, minds,—notwithstanding the irreverent scoffs of shallow sciolists,—that a knowledge of its apocatastatic whereabouts may be, to any age or nation, of unspeakable practical value; may I, benevolent reader, in your opinion, hope to be pardoned, if pardon it need, for what, doubtless to many, may look like a very presumptuous attempt, viz: the philanthropic attempt to point out to this age, and to this nation especially, its true apocatastatic relations to the past.

First of all, then, is the present, a fertile period in the Platonic sense, or is it a period of sterility; that is, according to Plato's own commentary upon himself, a period of dissolution, degeneracy, and corruption ($\varphi\theta o\rho\alpha$)? It is to be remembered that the baleful influence of the conjunction of malignant stars extends to animals, and plants, and to all social institutions, as well as to men personally. (See Repub. Lib. viii.) To begin with the vegetable kingdom,—witness the late Irish famine; and do not the dealers in flour already announce the approach of another? and more than ten famines, as likely to result in a standing famine, and, a thousand years hence to stand forth as the great historic event characteristic of the present times; witness the potato-rot!! Besides, all men must have observed that certain species of trees, in all places, and in all circumstances, seem to be struck with a fatal blight, as if a curse had been pronounced upon their race. Witness also the exorbitant prices of all articles of human food, that infallible criterion of scarcity: and I think that, without further proof, it must be acknowledged that the present is anything but a fertile period for the vegetable, and of course for the animal world. For can beasts flourish without browse, or men be prolific without potatoes? In regard to the human race moreover,—witness that terrible, and so often repeated scourge, of Cholera, and the hitherto unusual extent and malignity of yellow fever; and are not these sufficient evidence of the moral as well as of the physiological degeneracy and corruption of the present race of men? And, then, consider the institutions of the present; are not all the thrones of the old world trembling like an aspen in the wind, or at least so aguishly disposed that they shake "at the shaking of a leaf?" and are not we on the very verge of the dissolution of the Union? All things tend to change, that is, to dissolution, decay, corruption; it is manifest therefore, that we have entered upon one of Plato's periods of sterility.

What historic period, then, is calculated to remind us of the present time? of what period have the characteristic features and lineaments a strong family resemblance to those of the present? Do not all men of historic reading turn at once to the latter times of the Roman Republic? Has there ever been on earth any other republic with which our own can be for a moment paralleled? Thanks to Plutarch, and Mr. Thomas Taylor, we know that that also was a period of sterility, and also, still more fortunately, the very apocatastatic point of time at which it commenced; for it would avail us very little to know to what apocatastatic period we have succeeded, unless we can also ascertain in what part of its orbit we are now situated. But in order to arrive at this indispensable condition of available knowledge, it becomes necessary to determine also when the succeeding period, that is our own, had its commencement. From what date, now—or have we any date, from which to settle so nice a point of chronology? I fear we shall not be able to find any record of the repetition of that loud and *mournful* sound of a trumpet "on a cloudless and clear day," which heralded the birth, and indicated the exact moment of the advent, of our apocatastatic elder brother, (that is, provided we prove our relationship). And had there been such,—unless we are further advanced into the period than I incline to think,—beyond all doubt, the second advent people would not have failed to make a *note* of it. It is not however necessary, as I understand the Tuscan wise men, that identically the same wonderful sign should present itself at the ushering in of each corresponding period, but only that some equivalent sign should manifest itself from the earth or the heavens. It is recorded by the elder Pliny, (Natur. Histor. Lib. ii. 58) who also mentions the sound of the trumpet spoken of by Plutarch, that, about the same time, there was heard in the sky sounds as of a battle, and that armies were actually seen to approach each other and fight in the heavens. Now unless I remember incorrectly, it was recorded not more than thirty years ago, that, "on a cloudless and clear day" as I believe, there was heard in the heavens a pretty smart cannonading, and I think armies were seen also at this time. The portent was supposed, at the time, if I remember, to have some relation to some of the Creek or Seminole wars, while in fact it might have been intended to announce much more important events. But as this "sign," though perhaps as "wonderful," is not quite as well attested as that recorded by Pliny and Plutarch, it will not perhaps be safe to rely *wholly* upon it as a chronological, or apocatastatical, starting point, on an occasion of so much importance.

How, then, shall we find our initial point? A sarcastic whig proposes a solution of the difficulty which looks extremely plausible, and which, so far as I know, does not violate any law of interpretation laid down for such cases. I am so well pleased with his theory that I propose to adopt it, but as I am not a fighting man, in case I should, instead of being, in the usual slang, newspaper way, *called upon,* be politely *called out,* to defend it, I expect he will have the goodness to take my place. He says, then, that Sylla, being a consummate general and Consul, that is president of the Roman Republic, is to be considered a historical, or representative character, and that, as the period of sterility to which our own may prove to be second, is known to have begun in his time, we must, therefore, look for some corresponding representative individual of our own time. That is, we must find some individual holding equivalent offices in the Republic, and whose public or representative acts, moreover, correspond to those of Sylla. What, then, did Sylla? My friend says that he began "new measures" in the State by putting to death two of his enemies, or those who were setting on his enemies;—he does not say whether they were hanged,—that he first set the example of proscription, for opinion's sake, on a large scale ; that he made himself Dictator ; that he trampled not only on his enemies, but on all the other departments of the government ; and that, instead of executing the *laws,* he administered the *constitution,* as he understood it. And I think it must be confessed that history bears him out. He says moreover, with a lurking smile, which is rather a sneer, as if he himself may perhaps have been among the proscribed, that it is no slight confirmation of the correctness of his theory, that there has been an individual in our time, holding the same offices, and in all his public acts and relations copying so exactly *this* "old Roman," that, even without naming him, there is not a man in the United States who does not at once recognize the portrait; that the public character and conduct of the one are so perfect a counterpart of those of the other, that it is impossible to account for it except on the supposition of an apocatastatic "damnable iteration." Here, then, we have been enabled, with apparent certainty, to fix upon exactly corresponding and coincident points in the two periods, which, of course, determines their chronological relations throughout; for any other such points are equally available for that purpose as the initial points. We may, therefore, feel quite independent of any "certain wonderful sign," either from the earth or the heavens, as it is no longer of consequence to us whether it was accurately observed and recorded or not. Let us now suppose, for the present, that the historic and representative acts of our "old Roman" president are really, what they are apparently, apocatastatic copies, or repetitions, and we have not only coincident points of the two periods having apocatastatic relation, but those points are obviously—if any one may feel curious in that regard,—very near their respective beginnings; probably a little posterior, for the "mournful sound of the trumpet," according to Pliny, was heard during the Cimbric war, which was some years before the first consulship of Sylla, and this also is not at all discordant with the time mentioned by Plutarch; and we are prepared for a somewhat more detailed comparison and parallelism of the two periods assumed, to see whether they can really make out their apocatastatic identity. And first, and most strikingly characteristic, standing out from the historic canvass, obvious even to the blind, are the two grand, haughty, all-absorbing, overshadowing, Republics!! The thoughtful reader will also take note that these Republics are not only wonderfully parallel in all their *essential* relations—for how they may have happened to be in different parts of the earth has already been explained,—but also that they are unique, having no similarity to anything except to each other;—for their third preceding advent lies beyond the horizon of history, with the Trojan wars &c., "before Agamemnon," devoured, record and all, by that old Saturn, who, swine like, eats up his own offspring.

In their attitude towards, and treatment of, other nations

and governments, how are these Republics, as it were, the reflected images of each other. To compare here only characteristic traits and actions,—which will be sufficient,—did no Gen. Jackson whip the British in a pitched battle, as Sylla did Mithridates? did not another of our great generals conquer and reduce to a province of the Republic a great part of Mexico, as Caesar did Gaul? and as the Romans gained extensive possessions beyond the Alps and the Rhine, so have not we beyond the Rocky Mountains and the Rio del Norte and as the Romans insulted all the Kings of the East, eve the "Great King," so have not we bearded, and snubbed, th emperor of Austria, and called the Czar by opprobriou names? and as the Romans welcomed rebels from other State and received from them accusations against their own goveri ments, so do not we? and as the kings of the former perio *trembled,* at the very name of *Rome,* so dares the preser batch more than open its mouth and *peep,* at *us?*

Consider also the commerce of the ancient republic. At period a little posterior to the time of Sylla, how immense, t supply the incredible luxury of Italy, must have been, by tl way of Alexandria and the Red Sea, the traffic with India and are we not about to parallel that traffic with the san countries by the way of San Francisco and the Pacific, supply the same insatiable vanity and gluttony?

So much for the foreign relations of our illustrious prede cessor. And if we examine the two States interiorly we shall find the resemblance not less striking. In the ancient Repul lic, especially after that *"mournful* sound of the trumpet announced the period of sterility, corruption and decay, wha weary and sickening selfishness, mutual proscription, and utter annihilation of all patriotism in the politicians of all parties who floated, like scum upon dirty water, on the surface of the body politic! This state of political morality, we may say of all morality, was happily characterized by the convenient phrase, "omnia venalia Romae," all things, and all men. had their price, and were in the market at the servic highest bidder. Here too, alas!—my whig friend says from the time of the man who walked, step for step, track for track in the footprints of Sylla the Dictator,—the parallel is so disgustingly complete and perfect, that we can only point to it and exclaim, with averted face, mournfully as that solemn trumpet could have uttered its warning note: alter et idem! alter et idem! another yet the same! another yet the same!

At the same time, what a development there was of the adaptive faculty, of what may be called the *science of contrivance*, that instinctive tact which provides for the indolent ease, and convenience, of a rich and luxurious people; its products so splendid and gorgeous, so magnificent, and in many respects, so exquisitely comfortable—at least for those who were not employed in putting up the fixings,—that they must be supposed to have been patented, certainly some of them, in a part of the period at which we have not yet quite arrived.— And then, in regard to public improvements and facilities; on what a grand scale were they projected, and with what scientific precision and perfection finished, in those days. Witness their broad highways, constructed of solid mason-work, threading in all directions the republic and its provinces, extending even *to the far western ocean*, passing through mountains, and across largest streams by bridges which still remain; their aqueducts, by which whole rivers were made to flow, high above the surface of the earth, and pour their limpid treasures into the "eternal," and other cities; and also their associate washing, and soapsaving, establishments, called public baths, at that time. And are not we competing with them, though yet not fully, in all these, and such like particulars? and do we not christen ourselves the "Age of Progress," exclusively because of our "going ahead" in these very same directions? Though our road has not yet reached the western ocean.

If we look still more interiorly into the everyday life of our great prototype we find there as here, then as now, that most incredible of all meeting of extremes, men resenting with the most indignant pride and haughty jealously the least en croachment upon their freedom, surrounded by, and domineering over, with the most relentless tyranny, men whom they had deprived of all personal liberty. The highest freedom delighting in, and reposing upon the foul bosom of, the lowest slavery!! what a paradox then! what a paradox now! Then, as now, they had their foreign slave trade; then, as now, their domestic slave trade also;—and ah! how many parallels to the most touching and tragic tales of "Uncle Tom," and his "Key," then lacked a historian.

But more interior still, and infinitely more important, as underlying, modifying, and to a great extent controling, and giving their essential character to, all other relations, is the *religious* relation of men. Under which general term is to be included the sum of their belief and opinions, both positive and negative, not only in regard to their moral responsibility, and future or present accountability to a Divine Judgment seat and Judge or Judges, and in regard to their practical duties to Him or to them, to God, or to "the gods;" but also in regard to their relations to other spiritual beings of whatever kind, superhuman, infrahuman, or extrahuman, or to the disembodied, or unembodied, spirits of men. The opinions and belief of men in regard to this class of relations are the foundation and substratum, or rather the specific germ, of the whole *human* life, both of the individual man, and of communities and states. "The seeds" of all outward acts and conduct, not pertaining to the mere animal life, "descend from thence." "Here," some one will interpose and say; "here, Mr. Author, your parallel altogether fails, or comes short." Not too fast, my impatient reader, just here it is, on the contrary, in my opinion, that the parallel is most complete. For what was the characteristic, all inclusive, overshadowing theological dogma of the ancient times we are speaking of? "Jupiter est quodcunque vides." And of this deification of the all, the deification of the parts, was a perfectly natural consequence; that is, pantheism leads inevitably to polytheism. Accordingly, the ancients worshiped the Powers of nature, under various forms, and with various rites, consonant to their supposed attributes. And is not pantheism in our time also, proclaimed from high places, and from low places, and practically believed in, in all places, and by the same name of "Nature" under which it was formerly veiled ? The Powers of Nature too, somewhat better known perhaps than in the former period, and coerced to do the bidding of man by a stronger magic than that of the ancient theurgists, still, are they not equally *believed in*, trusted in, worshiped, in fact, and equally as in the ancient time, to the exclusion of the idea of a God to whom could be offered truly spiritual homage ? and have we not the same natural result, viz : the same essential atheism ? for pantheism, polytheism, and atheism, are reciprocally cause and effect, and are equivalent terms, or rather the same thing under different names, or Atheism is the identity or middle term, of which Pantheism and Polytheism are the extremes. In regard to our supposed relations to other spiritual beings, especially to disembodied spirits, or the spirits of dead men, the parallel is, if possible still more perfect. The ancients believed that the souls of the dead had much power and influence in human affairs, and that they could communicate with the living in various ways. The Romans therefore had their household divinities, which were the spirits of their dead ancestors, presiding over the fortunes of the family, and which could be consulted in case of doubt or difficulty by their descendants. They had, besides, inunmerable oracles of the dead, fanes, temples, where the spirits of particular, distinguished individuals, could, at any time, give response in regard to things present or future. In addition to these sources of information from the "spirit world," there were men and women, numerous as the spawn of Egypt, they were, in fact, in great part, the spawn of Egyt, by whose aid all sorts of spirits could be evoked and consulted at the pleasure of the questioner. Is there a parallel to all this in our own time? or is it an identity, the same thing ?—"Monsieur Tonson come again ?" For are not we coming to have; for each family; our guardian spirits? some father, brother, wife, or child, or all of them together, who can comfort and advise us? Have we not oracles where the spirits of great men are constantly consulted? and for those who can anywhere evoke the vulgar dead, could they have been more numerous in old Rome, or even in Egypt itself? Here truly are apocatastatic evidences to which I think no candid lawyer can demur. And, on the whole, are not the arguments which go to prove the present period, commencing at the time before spoken of,—for I do not wish to be offensively definite on that point,—apocatastatic of that beginning a little before the first consulship of Sylla, amply and abundantly conclusive? We know that the ancient period was one of sterility from the *mournfulness* of the sound of the trumpet, which indication could also be fully confirmed if necessary, but no reader of history will need any confirmation of it. We have seen too that the present period is one of sterility and corruption in the Platonic sense. And then, taking the two great republics as the central points of the two periods; how numerous, how striking, how identical, how wonderful, are the coincidences of the two periods thus far! their discrepancies, how few, how slight, how easily accounted for, if they were of sufficient importance to be accounted of. Surely, and beyond question, if there is not an apocatastatic relation here, there is plainly, no such thing as apocatastatic relations at all. But if the two periods under consideration have really such a relation to each other, (and who can longer doubt it?) and our own is to continue, as of course it is to continue, its parallelism with its predecessor; then, my countrymen, to what a future, Dii avertite omen, are we to look forward!! What seditions, revolts, rebellions, servile wars, civil wars, and other internecine strifes, are before us! what luxury, corruption, indolence, cowardice, vice, crime, impiety, and superstition, are to fall naturally and justly, under the terrible power of such a loathsome, and shameful, yet shameless despotism, as, surely, the earth is never polluted with, under the conjunction and influence of any other set even of misanthropic and malignant stars. Meantime, men, grown desperate, and hopeless of help from their gods, turn more and more to daemons and impious invocation of the dead, as if, deserted of heaven, and despairing of aid from thence, they would fain compel hell itself to their assistance; having come to believe and hope in lying spirits which a profane curiosity prompted them with unhallowed rites to consult. "But (these divine men) conceived the last period to be under the dominion of Mercury, to whom the Moon in the last place conjoins herself. What can be found more subtile than this arrangement? For mankind being purified from rude and savage pursuits, arts also having been invented, and disciplines disposed in an orderly manner, *the human race sharpened its inventive power.* And because the noble genius in man could not preserve (uniformly) one course of life, the improbity of evil increased from various institutes, and confused manners and the crimes of a life of wickedness prevailed: hence the human race in this period both invented and delivered to others more enormous machinations. On this account these wise men thought that this last period should be assigned to Mercury, so that, in imitation of that star, the human race might give birth to inventions replete with evil." (Firmicius, Mathesis,) Certainly, Mercury, the god of the merchants, is the Ruler of our period, the god also of the instinctive understanding by whose inspiration the human race has sharpened its inventive power to a most vulpine and wily sharpness, having renounced faith in all higher divinities. And are we not fast entering that part of our orbit where "the seeds" of "more enormous machinations, and inventions replete with evil," having already taken root, are about to perfect their fruit?

But is this hideous approaching night, of more than Egyptian darkness, left orbless, and without a ray, from the angry skies? lo! still beneath the eastern verge, one pitying Star throws up again its mild redeeming light, and the sinful earth is not wholly forsaken of heaven!

Thus much may suffice for the general parallel of the two periods, in regard, both to what is past, of our own, and to what is yet future. I hope however, it may not prove altogether uninteresting, just at the present time, or unprofitable, to the thoughtful reader, if, in one particular, viz: that of *intercourse of the living with the dead,* including its cognate subjects and their attendant manifestations, I shall follow the parallel somewhat more into detail, that we may determine, whether something has, indeed, at last, happened, "whereof it may be said, " See! this is new," giving the lie to the wisdom of Solomon; or whether we also must confess with him; "it hath been already of old time, which was before us." And in a moral and practical point of view, the subject of such intercourse may have another aspect, for some minds, if it shall prove to be only paganism come round again; than it presents, while they look upon it as some hitherto unknown, unique, and altogether peculiar, development of Nature or of Providence, reserved as the crowning boon for this, in-all-directions, especially backwards, progressive, and expansive age. Before entering upon the comparison in detail, however, it will be necessary, for the sake of the unlearned reader, in order that he may the better understand quotations and allusions hereafter to be made, to exhibit a very general outline of some of the ancient doctrines in regard to the character, power, and possible influence and participation in human affairs, of several classes of spiritual beings, and especially of the spirits of the dead. We shall then be prepared to enter upon a serious subject,—certainly from some points of view sufficiently serious,—I hope, with all due, and becoming, seriousness. Meanwhile, kind reader, excuse the seeming levity of the introduction, and take these preinitial chapters, this apocatastatic prelude,—so it be good-naturedly,—in whatever sense may best accord with your own astrologic whereabouts.

CHAPTER III.

Quum multae res in philosophia nequaquam satis adhuc explicatae sunt, tum perdifficilis, et perobscura quaestio est de natura Deorum * * * * * Plerique Deos esse dixerunt. * * * * Qui vero Deos esse dixerunt, tanta sunt in varietate ac dissentione, ut eorum molestum sit dinumerare sentendas.

Cicero, De Natur. Deor. Lib. i. C. 1.

Many things in philosophy are as yet by no means well understood; but, especially, the question concerning the nature of the Gods is one of great difficulty, and very obscure. * * * * * Most men believe in the existence of Gods. * * * * * * * * But of those who hold that there are Gods, the opinions in regard to them are so various and discordant that it were no small labor merely to count them.

Most of the heathens, it would seem, were not as "perfect converts in every particular" to their religion, even "as it was understood and illustrated by the Pythagoric and Platonic philosophers," as Mr. Thomas Taylor, the Platonist; and among these we may reckon Cicero himself, though he also was so much of a Platonist that, "he would rather be wrong with Plato than right with anybody else." If the opinions of the ancients concerning the Gods were so numerous that it would be no small undertaking just to enumerate them, I shall not, of course, be expected to exhibit them all, or even many of them, on the present occasion. Indeed, were this in my power, the purposes of this tract do not require more than the most general outline of some of the leading hypotheses. The two most important theories were those of emanation, and of evolution, which, taking their starting points from opposite extremes, met each other half way in a common polytheism. Both held to the eternity of matter, and the emanation theory to the co-eternity of spirit also. It commenced from "the good," or "the one." "The principle and first cause of all things is the good; and the good itself is the same with the one" says Proclus. But this one, because of his perpetual exuberance, remains not a mere barren entity, but immediately proceeds into Being, or *Being itself*, which is no other than the *highest order of the gods*, otherwise expressed as *Intellect itself*, or the intelligible world, or the divine Paradigm, or Exemplar of the Universe, where all variety and multitude are contained potentially, or in "occult union." But it is necessary that this occult multitude should be expanded into actual diversity, hence a third procession originates, in which multitude no longer subsists indivisibly, but is perfectly diffused in order to the actual diversity of things, and the existence of the sensible world. This third principle is no other than *Soul*, which expands the impartibility of Intellect, and unfolds all that was involved in its unity. After these three Principles there remains nothing but the gradation and diversities of multitude. But we are still very high up in the series, we have not yet descended to the furthest and outermost Stars; for this Soul is not yet the anima mundi, or Soul of the world, but is the Supermundane Soul, the Demiurgus, or Fashioner of the visible Universe by impressing upon preexistent matter the form of the intelligible Paradigm as near as the perversity of the material would admit; and by procession into it from himself, of a lower grade of Soul than himself, which is the "Soul of the world." Am I right, Mr. Taylor? But still far and steep is the way to this "terrene abode," and to "the last of things;" it will be safest therefore

for us to take the strong hand of some one well acquainted with the path. "Having thus fabricated the body of the
" Universe a perfect whole from perfect parts, he placed in its
" center a Soul, and caused it to pervade the body through its
" whole extent, and also to infold it from without. * * * * * *
" and so, from all these causes, he generated a blessed God.
" He also formed our nurse the Earth, the first and oldest of
" the Gods generated within the celestial sphere. Of Earth
" and Heaven the children are Oceanus and Tethys, of these
" Phocys, Saturn, and Rhea, and whoever is of that series ; of
" Saturn and Rhea, Jupiter and Juno and their brothers, and
" those who are descended from these. After these, and next
" to these, are Daemons who inhabit the air, *are always near*
" *us, though commonly invisible to us, and know all our*
" *thoughts.* They are intermediate between gods and men,
" their function is to interpret and convey to the gods what
" comes from men, and to men what comes from the gods. All
" intercourse and conversation between gods and men are car-
" ried on by means of daemons. When, therefore, all the
" Gods which revolve visibly in heaven, and those which ren-
" der themselves visible when they please, were created, the
" Generator of this *All* thus addressed them. Gods of gods,
' there are three mortal races yet to be formed, without which
" heaven will not be perfect. That this universe, therefore
" may be indeed a Universe, betake yourselves according to
" your nature to the formation of animated beings, imitating
" the power which was exercised in your own production. So
" saying, he poured into the same vessel as before, the remain-
" der of the materials from which the Soul of the world was
" formed, and tempering them nearly in the same manner as
" before, though with only the second and third degree of pu-
" rity, he finished the whole, and drew out and distributed
" Souls to each of the stars, and showing them the Universe,
" he announced to them the laws of their existence ; that it
" was necessary they should descend into bodies possessed of
" various passions ; that he who controled them by reason, and

"lived virtuously should return to his appropriate star and
"lead a happy life; but that he who obeyed passion and lived
"unjustly should return into another body and be born a wo-
"man, (Oh! Rev. Miss Brown, what enormities were you
guilty of in your preceding life, when you were, bona fide, of
the masculine gender!!) and if that was not enough to re-
"form him he should next be born a beast. Having made
"known to them the law, he scattered them in the Earth, the
"Moon, and other instruments of time, and commanded the
"junior gods to fashion mortal bodies and unite them to human
"souls, and to rule over and govern in the best manner the
"mortal creature, except in so far as he might be the author
"of evil to himself." (Plato, in Timaeus, and other Dialogues.)
Here we have a procession, gradation, of pre existent spirit
until it descends into, and impresses its forms upon pre-existent matter, that receptacle and nurse of all generation.
(πασης γενεσεως υποδοχην)

The opposite theory begins where the Pythagorico-Platonic
hypothesis ends, with an eternal matter; not, however, the
same passive receptivity as in the other case, waiting to be
acted upon. Motion was a part of its definition. It needed
only room enough, a vacuum, κενον, to work in. Having found
space, and set itself to circumgyrating, each atom seeking its
private fortune, and meeting at length with some fellow atom,
compounds, or rather concretes, were formed, but whence the
law of affinity or cohesion does not appear. It must of course
have been latent in the atoms. Thus the four elements, fire,
air, earth, water, were arrived at. From this point there could
be no difficulty, and the universe evolved itself somehow, em-
pirically, though not as fast probably, as it was, in the other
case, constructed by the "father of works." But, not having
any paradigm to work by, some of its seeming mistakes may
be the more readily accounted for. Thus, in due time, were
evolved the earth, sun, moon, stars, planets, plants, fishes, in-
sects, quadrupeds, monkeys, men, demons, gods, mundane and
supermundane, for aught that appears, quite up to the "super-

essential one;" the evolution ending where the Pythagoric emanation begins. Certainly quite a remarkable accident with all its misfortuities. This is the most ancient development theory, this side of history, often since reappearing with variations, on the return of certain comets, and in our own time especially.

These theories, however, were, for the most part, the day-dreams of philosophers merely, rather accommodating themselves to popular opinion and practice than having much control over them. The origin of the everyday heathen theology with its rites is very obscure. What seems sufficiently certain is that its underlying idea was a kind of natural unconscious pantheism, in which it came nearest to the development theory; a sort of Nature-gods of every rank and quality, high and low, good and evil, from Jupiter optimus Maximus, to the infra-human subterranean elves, being evolved, and appearing everywhere, like electric sparks at metallic points. The sun, moon, planets, stars, earth, heaven, ocean, were divinities, as in the Platonic theology, besides those which presided over mountains, forests, groves, rivers, springs, countries, cities, towns, places, ("genius loci") caves, mines, and individual men. Their number was innumerable. Yet, lest there should be some not duly honored, there were also altars erected to the "unknown god." Besides all these, who could communicate with men directly or indirectly, the heathens everywhere worshiped, and constantly consulted, the spirits of the dead. Altogether a pretty liberal provision for intercourse with the *"spirit world,"* and for getting news from the *"spirit land,"* to use the slang phrases of the day.

In all the ancient theories, and especially in the popular belief, these beings were part good and part evil. In the Platonic theology there would seem to be no way for evil beings to originate except in the perversity, or rather imbecility, of matter. The universe and its parts, the celestial gods, have bodies in which, and over which, they, as it were, preside merely, for "the soul of the Universe is not bound by the things which it binds. For it has dominion over them. Hence it is not passively affected by them." That is, the bodies of the celestial deities do not excite passion in them. But the Demons of the middle region are the workmanship of the "junior gods," and their spiritual part came out of the second soul-mixture, and so is of a secondary quality. They have also bodies, of finer organization, however, than those of men, to which they are so united as to be subject to passion, and some of them exercise malignant passions. The development theory could of course evolve good and evil indifferently, and Plutarch says that Democritus himself, one of the chief authors of it, believed in both good and evil spirits. And the popular belief inclined perhaps, more to evil than good, so that most of their service was merely deprecatory. Much of this, however, undoubtedly, arose from the innate consciousness of moral accountability, and the feeling that the gods would be ultimately just. The spirits of the dead also were partly benevolent and partly malevolent towards their yet embodied descendants and fellow-men.

These beings, especially of the lower orders, were always present with men, commonly invisibly, sometimes visibly, influencing them in a great variety of ways, both for good, and for evil.

Their organs of more direct communication with men were, sometimes, the gods of elevated rank, but generally either the Demons of the intermediate region between gods and men; or, especially, the spirits of the dead.

The methods of intercourse between the two worlds, and of prying into futurity, were by means of Oracles, Omens, dreams, the lot, astrology, magical divination,—the ancient mesmerism,—aided by magical statues, tripods, rings, spheres, water, mirrors; and necromancy proper, or the evocation of, and direct conversation with, the spirits of the dead.

The intercourse, of these various kinds, was not uncommon and rare, but frequent, constant, and among the daily events of the ancient heathen life. "Chrysippus collected *innumerable* oracles (oracular responses) yet no one which was not confirmed by abundant authority and testimony." (Cicero, de Divinatione, lib. i.)

The gods however were not, with the exception of Apollo, very communicative in that way; much less so than the spirits of the dead. Oraculis *hoc genus* (that is of the dead) stipatus est orbis; says Tertullian, the world is crowded with them. He is speaking only of the public fanes and temples and of course does not include the "household gods" who were also spirits of the dead. These gods and spirits exercised incredible influence in human affairs, since nothing of consequence either public or private was undertaken without consulting them. The pleasure of the gods was also constantly consulted, especially among the Romans, by omens; the augurs, whose business it was to interpret them, being public officers of the state. Sortilege also, or consulting the *lot*, in various ways, was exceedingly common. But besides these public and legal and religious methods of searching into futurity,—for this was always the essential purpose of them,—the various forms of magical divination, including necromancy, which were private, forbidden by law, and commonly held to be profane and impious,—these, for sometime before and after the fall of the Roman Republic, were everywhere the rage, and contributed, no doubt, with other causes, to the neglect of the established oracles at that time; since we find men of all ranks, including the Emperors themselves, having recourse to these sacrilegious methods of gratifying their curiosity in regard to the future. The elder Pliny says that when this science was first introduced from the East, the Greeks took it up not merely with avidity but that they were *rabid* after it; that in his time it prevailed in almost all parts of the world; that inasmuch as there was no man who was not desirous of knowing the future in regard to himself, and who did not believe that such knowledge was most successfully to be sought from heaven;—that, *it therefore, made pretensions to religion,* in regard to which, however, it, more than anything else, (maxime,) *darkens the minds of men.* (caligat humanum genus.)

But it is high time, and more than time, the reader may think, to commence the promised parallel. This dull chapter, however, dear reader, may be of service to us hereafter, and as I hate words, it shall be my study in all things to be brief. I shall therefore, for your sake and my own, restrict the comparison about to be made between things presumed to be apocatastatically related, to certain theoretico-practical opinions; to certain practices, in regard to which I shall endeavor to show essential, but not always identical, sameness,—chiefly, to those which were anciently called magic, divination, enchantment, necromancy; and are now known by the names of magnetism, mesmerism, biology, physical manifestations, spirit-intercourse &c.; and to certain opinions in regard to the character, causes, and consequences of these practices and the resulting phenomena. And the parallel will be mostly or wholly, between properly ancient, and present times.

CHAPTER IV.

Αλλα μην υποληπτεον και την των ανθρωπων φυσιν πολλα και παντοια υ-
πο των αυτην περιεςωτων πραγματων διδαχθηναι τε και αναγκασθηναι.
Epicurus, apud Diogenem Laert. L. x.

APOCATASTATIC TRANSLATION.—" How is it possible for man to be "free," while pent up between two contending forces? Reason, the soul's prime minister, replies unequivocally in the negative; because man, materially, *and spiritually*, possesses universal affinities which he did not create, which he *cannot control*, which he cannot destroy; but he is compelled to *act as he is acted upon*." THE GREAT HARMONIA. Vol. ii. p. 225.

Such as is the Theoretic, or most general and fundamental view of the "nature of things," and of human relations, such are the practical opinions, and such again the conduct of men, whether of individuals, or of communities, or of periods.— And this, and these, again, are determined, and predetermined, to a great extent, by the *character*, that is, by the moral or voluntary character, of those who hold them; whether such views and opinions originate then and there, or whether, the "seeds" of them, "descending from the stars," or from some other superior or anterior point, find then and there, their fitting nidus, and appropriate soil. For all *practical* beliefs, —not mere inherited, professed, or pretended opinions, but

—all practical *beliefs* are, for the most part, matter of choice. And though they react, and often strongly, on the character of those who originate, or who adopt them, it were a question not easy to decide, whether they are more *cause* than *effect* of such character. What is quite certain is that they mutually act and react, each increasing and confirming the other. Hence it is found in all the languages of men, that, all men have ever, and as it were unconsciously, held each other morally responsible for their *practical* opinions. This truth, however, is so trite as to be often overlooked and forgotten; nay, it is even denied, oftentimes, by men who, slightly self-conscious, obstinately refuse to see, what is quite obvious to everybody but themselves, that they have mistaken for truth, the mere shadow of their own wishes. Certain principles, therefore, with their consequent opinions, are, as it were, connatural and appropriate to certain individuals, places, and periods, so that by some law of spontaneity, or equivocal generation, they emerge there, or however originating, do, in fact, come to take possession of the minds to which they are adapted; and persons, or periods, similar in character, will originate or adopt similar or equivalent principles and opinions. For man, however self-degraded to a brute, is ever more than a mere animal; his spiritual character asserts itself under all circumstances. No *man* acts wholly, like animals, by mere intelligent instinct or impulse. He must have "principles of conduct," implying more or less the idea of duty or spiritual obligation; and inasmuch as incompatibility of their conduct with their principles is, for all men, a relation in which they are ill at ease, a reconciliation is constantly aimed at, and by most men rather by adapting the principles to the conduct than the conduct to the principles. Or, if it is predetermined that the conduct shall have no relation to the law of duty, such determination will be accompanied by some theory which shall exclude from itself all recognition of such law of duty,—the spiritual asserting itself in the very act of denying its own existence.

The period, with which the present is to be compared, was one, of the most active intellectual development, conjoined with a most thorough, and almost total, corruption in politics and morals; relentless oppression yielding incredible wealth for the supply of a luxury more gorgeous and magnificent, and at the same time more dissolute and shameless, than the world had hitherto witnessed; manifesting such forms of vice and crime, that lower degradation, or greater wickedness, would seem to be impossible to man. In such a period, and for such men,—men of active minds, theorising, philosophising, speculating, in all directions, as if to find a reason or an apology to themselves for their conduct,—for such men, the Pythagorico-Platonic theology, which recognized a Maker, a Providence, and *spiritual* accountability, was, plainly, inappropriate. Such a period, and such men, could not originate, and would not adopt, principles demanding sobriety, honesty, morality, religion,—there could be no affinity, but only mutual antipathy and repulsion. Such an atheistic, or pantheistic, development theory, as that of Democritus, or of whatever more ancient day-dreamer, may have been the father of it,— if it be not rather the spontaneous offspring, *at all times*, of the minds of men who cannot tolerate the presence of a personal Deity who "taketh account" of human conduct,—*such* a theory was a seed much more likely to take root and bring forth fruit in such a soil. This theory, accordingly, after its Epicurean modification;——which, appeasing somewhat the Nemesis of conscience by admitting the existence of "the gods," while at the same time it represented them as wholly indifferent to human affairs,—became a more permanent and hopeless, because less disquieting, form of atheism, than the total denial of the existence of the Deity; and while it spoke beautifully of the beauty and pleasure of virtue and piety, as worthy to be practiced for their own sake, and of the happiness of conformity to the physical laws of man's organism, and so lulled the soul with a Syren-song,—for if happiness is the end, are not the means a matter of taste not to be disputed about? and what are the laws of the organism but the natural impulses of the organs?—by removing the only restraints which could control, and the only incitements to virtue which could influence, corrupt and wicked men, and by furnishing them, at the same time, with what they most of all desired, *principles*, conformable to their predetermined conduct, it made reformation hopeless by seeming to make vice both safe and reasonable. This theory, so modified, became the main source of the "principles of conduct" for the leading men of the period in question. What rendered this theory so acceptable and welcome to those already predisposed to receive it, was,—both before and after its modification,—its total abrogation of the law of duty, its practical denial of all properly spiritual accountability. For what cared the men of that period, what care the profligate and licentious, the vicious and the wicked, of any period, for mere physical responsibility to the violated "Laws of Nature," if any sophistry can even but half persuade them that the conscience which makes cowards of them, the fearful looking-for of future retribution at the hands of a personal, holy, and just Judge, are but the shadows of groundless fears, the uneradicated superstitions of the nursery? Let those embrace virtue who find her lovely; to them she is neither beautiful nor desirable; and are they not as much entitled to their choice of happiness as those who seek it in a different form? and if they sometimes carry their enjoyment to what some are pleased to call excess do they not at least make sure of it? if the Laws of Nature are offended have they not antidotes wherewith to appease, or can they not cheat, blind nature, or reform in time to prevent unpleasant consequences? Or if they deliberately prefer a short life and a merry one to the tedium of a stupid life of sobriety and virtue, have they not a right to choose for themselves? It was not so much its denial of a future life, which was a part of the modification of this theory, which part, however, comparatively few adopted, as it was its view of the "Nature of things," and of the character of the Gods, which made it so soothing and welcome an application to the conscience, and gave to it its peculiar influence. For the Gods were wholly removed from human affairs, and indifferent to human conduct, neither rewarding nor punishing them except by the physical consequences of their actions, and therefore the fear of death was effectually taken away, even for those who did not believe it to be the termination of existence. Such views of man's relation to the Deity, propagated by leading minds, and gradually pervading all ranks of men, must have reacted strongly to quicken the development of that kind of character which already demanded them. And of the correctness of such views what stronger confirmation could be given than such examples of successful wickedness, "unwhipt of justice," as that of Sylla, and of Augustus, and indeed of Rome herself, as the mistress of the world? Add to this the views of Nature which belonged to the same theory, as a machine setting itself in motion, or if set in motion by the gods, evolving, without their further care, whatever it may evolve,—a self-developing universe. Considering that it commenced as a chaos of indivisible atoms having only vague likings and dislikings, it had already done much; it had really become a very splendid and efficient piece of machinery, and what new products might not now be expected from it. For, according to this view, it was, plainly, no apocatastatic contrivance, everlastingly reiterating itself, and recurring to the same points,—else it never would have arrived at its present point of evolution,—but a progress in a straight line, evermore arriving at new regions. It had evolved man with his present life and why not a future life? had not Caesar, who was once known to cry like a sick girl "give me some drink," and "help me Cassius," become a god? and had not Caesar's horse come to be Consul? The human mind had been evolved to know much, of visible things, why not of invisible? it had explored in all directions the present life, why not the future? it could take knowledge of the distant in space, why not of the distant in time? did not the evolution manifestly tend to the convergence of all intelligence and power in man as the lord as well as the product of Nature? was not Rome the earthly Providence, and did not Caesar already hold divided empire with Jupiter? might there not be some magic word of power which would enable him to control, not only nature, but the gods themselves? which should compel all spirits, whether of unembodied or disembodied, men, of heroes, demons, gods, to make known their secrets, and to unfold to men the future? Such were some of the last results of the ancient theory of progress: so thought and so experimented our apocatastatic predecessors. (Plin. Nat. Hist. L. xxx. v.) A way of looking at the "nature of things" admirably adapted to keep alive curiosity, to awaken expectation, and to make credible whatever new and wonderful things might manifest, or seem to manifest, themselves; a way indeed, that might make doubly credulous credulity itself. Such, and such-like fundamental principles, in regard to the "nature of things," and in regard to the nature of the gods, together with the popular belief in regard to man's relations to the dead, and to other spirits, must have tended strongly, notwithstanding the Epicurean denial of the immortality of the soul, to produce that outburst of impious curiosity in regard to the future, attempting to satisfy itself by sacrilegious experiments in regard to man's power to evoke and compel spirits, which characterized the period under consideration; although, doubtless, the maddening excitements of political parties, and during the latter part of the period, at which *we* have not yet arrived, every man's fear for his life, which hung upon the caprice of a despot, must have super-added to curiosity, intense anxiety, to know, not only his own future, but that of his enemies also. Certain it is, that, during the last century of the Roman Republic, and the first centuries of the Empire, men seemed madly resolved, by whatever means, and at whatever cost, and hazard, to rend the veil which conceals the future from the present, though it were necessary to assault the heavens, or to make descent upon hell itself.

That our own period is not in all these respects yet quite

parallel to its predecessor may be true, but it is to be remembered that we are yet near its commencement. Our wealth is yet rapidly increasing, and so our luxury and consequent vices and crimes have not arrived at their acme. Our political parties have not yet quite reached the point where to the victors belong not only the spoils, but the lives, also, of the minority; and we are yet, it may be, a hundred years from the evolution of a Caesar, and the establishment of the Empire. But our business in the present chapter is with principles and opinions, and here I think we shall find the parallelism pretty fairly commenced. To say nothing of older pantheistic theories and pantheistic men, as Spinoza, Hobbes, &c., or of the atheistic spawn of Germany, not without their influence, direct or indirect, now and here; have we not, in our own time, and language, popular writers of highest talents, who with wide, deep, and insidious power, subvert the foundations of all proper human responsibility?—for pantheism, and the "Eternal Laws," know, or teach, only the responsibility appropriate to animals. Wide-spread, and fearful to the humanity in men is this influence. Witness, as a single specimen of it, in "The Life" of poor Sterling, a soul capable of the truest and fullest spiritual life and development, perishing in the serpent folds of atheistic sophistry, like an unhappy beast in the embrace of the anaconda.

As for development theories, which come next in the order of evolution after atheism,—for where there is no Creator the Universe must be gotten up in some other way,—O, Democritus, with what undreamed-of apocatastatic honors has your dreaming head been crowned! "a hundred sons and every son a god!" and competent, every one, to the highest functions of Deity. Well may these awaken expectation, as indeed they have. For instance, we are looking daily for the advent of the "New Man;" but whether to be evolved out of the old one, or in some more kindred line of development, as in that, it may be, of the innocent, non-carniverous, fruit-consuming Simiae—on this point we are in doubt. This we know, that oftentimes, of late, he has attempted to be born, of the old effete humanity, but though the throes are strong and even convulsive, they never prove sufficient to bring him to the birth.— The vis vitae of the race seems too weak for such a product. We may, therefore, among other things, expect that the sceptre is about to depart from our house. "The perfectibility of the human race," therefore, which our pride prompts us to believe in as the natural order of evolution, may prove a problem too hard for the outworking powers, and may compel them, in order to "progress," to recede and take another path, even as the Democritic atoms, as we are informed, and may well believe, tried innumerable combinations before they arrived at the present order of things. But I am wandering somewhat from my purpose, which was to show, that, the development theories of our time are sufficiently like those of the period we have been considering to have sprung from the same siderial semination or planting, that is, apocatastatically the same; and that they have had, and have, an analogous influence and effect. My limits, and promise to be brief, forbid the attempt to characterize, or even to name, all the recent specimens of world-manufacture; being not less numerous, or less admirable, than those of the renowned Knickerbocker Catalogue of Cosmogonies. They would be found equally so, probably, in the period to which ours has succeeded, were we to look for them in that curious old Patent Office to which ours also are rapidly hastening, the limbo of things lost. I shall only glance at one or two of them, which—incredible as the fact may seem, and indeed, were it not for the obvious truth of the observations with which this chapter commences, must appear, even to credulity herself,—which, I say, have been, and are, the source of principles of conduct, not merely of speculative principles, but of actual faith and practice, to men and women not a few. The Vestiges of Creation, which was a sort of nine days wonder in certain quarters, and, still lingers there in its effects, was doubtless the clever attempt of some literary Gulliver to measure the utmost dimensions of the gullibility of that self-complacent personage, the reading Public. But what must have been his astonishment, and amusement, at finding his line too short; at finding himself, instead of being laughed at as a scientific Munchausen, revered, as another Newton; at finding his dreams accepted and acted upon as realities! But though this theory, such theories, might well be reckoned not within the sphere of sober criticism, as indeed, they are not, in relation to the rational understanding, yet their influence for evil is not small in relation to the moral and spiritual convictions and practical conduct and duties of men. Their effect is two-fold. They disturb the logical understanding, and the feelings of many whose spiritual relations to the truth are right, but who are pained, disquieted, and sometimes thrown into distressing doubt, and fear, at suggestions which are mere puzzles to the faculty judging according to sense, or even at the bare possibility of mistake in regard to their faith in providence, in redemption, in immortality, and in God. What to them are the Eternal Laws, and Immutable Nature, and Free Development; what to them is all visible beauty, though Nature were ten times more beautiful? what to them the grandeur of Nature manifesting mighty power? what to them law, order, design, exhibiting perfect intelligence? what though taste and intellect find in full measure their satisfying correlatives; if, mean while, their highest *spiritual* intuitions and aspirations find not their corresponding object? if an eternally productive Principle, or Law of development, evolving certain beneficent results, and working out in some cases a sort of physical retribution, has taken the place of the Eternal Law-giver and Judge, whom they love in proportion as they fear, and fear in proportion as they love Him. What to them this Universal Nature, and magnificent dwelling for the earthly man, to whom God is but an Instrument, and to whom therefore Nature is sufficient, if the spiritual life find not Him who is its End.

To those, on the contrary, a much more numerous class, to whom the presence of God is disquieting and unwelcome, to whom the consciousness of moral responsibility, and the belief of future retribution, are a weary restraint upon *their* free development, who will gladly acknowledge their accountability to the Laws of Nature, so they may escape the scrutiny of an omniscient and just Sovereign,—as undutiful children rejoice to be left to the care of servants,—to these, such theories as exclude from the Universe a personal Deity, or, what is equally satisfactory, admit only a Soul of the world, or some Epicurean Divinity, remote, and indifferent to human conduct, or who leniently expunges *sin, wicked,* and such-like ungentlemanly terms from his vocabulary, and good-naturedly finds men only frail, erring, or unfortunate—such theories, to such men, are not only welcome, but, however they may outrage, both reason and understanding, and the deepest consciousness of mankind, they are, to a great extent, practically believed in, or at least serve as a pretext, and seeming source of principles, for the course of conduct already chosen, and so remove, or diminish, that restless disquiet of a wholly unappeased conscience, whose tendency was to drive them towards the truth.

But, of all the recent theories of development and progress, that which seems to have most influence at present, especially in relation to the peculiar apocatastatic movement which it is the main purpose of this tract to consider, is entitled "The Principles of Nature." It may, indeed, by the fairest analogy, be reckoned the Epicurean modification of the Vestiges of Creation. In its coarse materialism, and in its moral aspect and bearings, with its incessant small-talk of virtue and benevolence, while it saps the whole foundation of human virtue, it is strictly, and even plagiaristically, Epicurean. It has simply superadded to the Epicurean theory what it calls the immortality of the soul, but which would more properly be called the eternal mortality of the soul, for it is only its mortal life prolonged. By making man, body and soul,—for spirit by the theory he has none,—the material product of material forces and manipulations, a kind of chemico-mechanical result,—*material* Laws!! think of that ye meditating atoms,—and subjecting him wholly, and only, to the laws of Nature, it divests him of all distinctive humanity, and makes him simply,—snatching the sceptre from the Lion's grasp,—the "King of Beasts." By denying to man all moral character and responsibility, all spiritual relations of course cease to exist; conscience is only the product of priestcraft, God is only the soul of the world, and man holds the same relation to him,—or to *it* rather,—as a tree, or mineral, except that the evolution in him of the quality of locomotion, and the distillation of a very refined and subtile matter called prudence, or forethought, render him, in a somewhat different way from that of the tree, physically accountable for the physical relations in which he voluntarily places himself. Religion there can be none; and the "progress" of the human animal, as indicated by the theory, is such, that the wolves among them would, in due time, in this world or the next, become good household dogs, tigers would be transformed to domestic cats, the large fishes would cease to eat the small ones, the hawks to devour the chickens, the crows to pull what they did not plant, and ultimately all would arrive at a most comfortable zoological paradise. This, it must be acknowledged, is a step beyond Epicurus, by the addition of plenty of time for the proposed progress; but, unluckily for the theory, the progress of most persons is in the opposite direction, from better to worse, but this is mostly owing to religion, circumstances will, doubtless, be more favorable in the next sphere, where there is probably no religion, as there will be none here when this theory is universally adopted. His admirers may then appropriate to the author of it the triumphant language of the great commentator upon Epicurus in regard to him;

—Omne immensum peragravit mente animoque,
Unde refert nobis victor, quid possit oriri,
Quid nequeat; finita potestas denique quoique
Quâ nam sit ratione, atque alte terminus haerens.

*Quâ re Religio, pedibus subjecta, vicissim
Obteritur, nos exæquat victoria cœlo.*
                  Lucretius De Rerum Natura, Lib. i. 75–80.

With clairvoyant vision he surveyed immensity, returning thence triumphant, laden for us with rich spoils, to wit: the power to know what events are possible, and what are impossible; the law of each finite evolution; and what yet remains latent and undeveloped; *whereby Religion, trampled in the dust, is, in its turn, vanquished; the victory places us on equal terms with heaven.*" This language is quite as applicable to the author of the Principles of Nature, and of the Great Harmonia, as to Epicurus himself; at least in the peculiar mental regions where his influence is felt, as it is just now pretty extensively. The essential quality of these theories, the same in both, which renders them so inviting to nine tenths of those who would fain believe them, and do practically *believe in them,* is the delightful anodyne to the conscience which they administer, the deliverance from the heavy incubus of religion, and from the bondage of the fear of death, which they bestow, and the liberty which they confer, of free, spontaneous, development, without the chilling drawback of a future account to give. For if there be no God, or if the "Divine Nature" sit apart in careless self-enjoyment,

"Ipsa suis pollens opibus, nihil indiga nostri,
Nec bene promeritis capitur, nec tangitur irâ,
                Lucretius De Rerum Natura, Lib. i. 61-2.

itself sufficient to itself, desiring nothing of us, and neither regards our virtues, nor is displeased at our vices;" what a delightful relief to many men, if not to most men, to believe that they are thus free to make the most of nature, every man according to his taste, responsible only to nature; and that they may thus have the full enjoyment of whatever their talents and tastes may enable and prompt them to compass and acquire, unmitigated, and unalloyed, by the uninvited presence of any horrid Nemesis, or by the intrusive thought of a judgment to come. Not that those who are disposed to adopt atheistic, or rather, rathumotheistic theories, are always persons of more than ordinarily depraved or vicious character ; on the contrary they are often men of amiable and benevolent disposition, quite exemplary, it may be, in regard to the second commandment,—though assuredly very little developed in the consciousness of their spiritual relations,—who in discarding or enervating the idea of retribution, are thinking rather of its relation to others, than to themselves ; but even to such, their theory, in proportion as they really believe in it, is like an emergence from gloom and shadow to a warmer and more cheering light ; for to those who know not, or love not, above all things, the religion which exhibits the character of God as elevated above all human thought, and unyielding as fate itself, in its moral attributes,—to such, this religion is, and has ever been, that gravis Religio,

Quae caput a coeli regionibus obtendebat,
Horribili super adspectu mortalibus instans.
Lucretius de Rerum Natura, Lib. i. 65-6.

Her head who high towards heaven uplifting proud,
With dreadful aspect frowns on mortal men.

These theories of mere nature-evolution, and, of course,— except in a physical sense—of irresponsible development for man, and of ever new unfolding, and upliftings of the veil of Nature, to be expected—this expectation more sparingly expressed in the ancient theory, though equally implied there as in the modern, for if nature has evolved thus much after infinite experiments, what reason to suppose that she intends no more experiments ? indeed Lucretius expressly says,

Sic igitur mundi naturam totius ætas
Mutat, et ex alio terram status excepit alter ;
Quod potuit nequeat ; possit, quod non tulit ante.

(Lib. v. 832-4) which Good translates more correctly than common ;

"So time transmutes the total world's vast frame,
From state to state urged on, now void of powers
Erst known, and boasting those unknown before."

—these theories of evolution and expectation, and all essentially godless, though they may not have given birth, at least not wholly, to the opinions and practices of their respective periods, which are about to be compared; certainly have promoted them, both by removing all moral restraint in regard to practices, many of which in all times have been commonly held to be impious; and by awakening, or stimulating, especially in the modern instance, a vague, restless and at the same time, profane curiosity. Such views of nature, and of man's relation to God, in concert with the, anciently, widespread, and in the present period, widely spreading, notions in regard to man's relations to disembodied spirits, certainly were, and are, a fitting preparation, in the minds of those who admit them, for the spirit-fanaticism, the epidemic necromancy, and other methods of divination, which are characteristic alike, both of the ancient, and the present periods.

CHAPTER V.

"He holds him with his glittering eye—
The wedding-guest stood still,
And listens like a three years' child,
The Mariner hath his will."

THE ANCIENT MARINER.

The ancients were, undoubtedly, well acquainted with the phenomena which are the result of what is now called mesmerism, biology, clairvoyance &c.; and which were then the effect of the same causes known by the names of fascination, enchantment, divination, magic, &c. The power thus acquired by one person over another was probably made use of for unlawful purposes, since the practice of these impious arts, as they were then accounted, was forbidden on pain of death. That the ancients knew how to produce mesmeric effects by the eye alone is often implied, and not very unfrequently expressed, by contemporary authors. This was called fascination, (fascinatio, βασκανια, as if from φαεσσι καινειν, to kill with the eyes) though this word was not appropriated exclusively to effects produced by the eye. Certain kinds of praise which were intended to injure, and were supposed to prove pernicious to, their object, were called also fascination. Not in the sense in which we sometimes speak of one being fascinated and spoiled, by flattery or excessive praise; but the notion was precisely the same as still exists in Eastern countries where mothers, in evident alarm, snatch their children from the presence of strangers who express admiration of them. It seems difficult to conjecture the origin of such an opinion, the ground of such fears, unless we suppose that the praise was considered as a kind of lure, while the child was being brought under the power of the "evil eye." Something more than this, however, is implied in the following quotation, since we can hardly suppose inanimate objects to be injured by any neuropathic effects. "Isigonus and Nymphodorus assert that there are certain families in Africa who have the power of fascination by praise (laudatione)—that whatever is praised by them perishes,—*trees wither*—children die." (Plinii Natur. Histor. Lib. vii. 2.) From the time of the elder Pliny to the present is a pretty long period for a wholly groundless notion to have sustained itself. "Isigonus adds that there are persons of the same kind among the Treballians and Illyrians, who fascinate *by the eye also*, and that they even cause the death of those upon whom they look long and intently, especially if with an expression of anger; and that the young more readily feel their pernicious influence." (Idem Ibidem.) Appollonides also relates that there are women of this sort in Scythia. Phylarchus says there are many possessed of a similar power in Pontus." (Idem Ibidem.) These quotations show expressly that the mesmeric power of the eye was anciently well known and exercised; the following *imply* the same thing, in such-wise as to furnish equally strong proof of its existence. "Why do we as a defence against fascination use a peculiar form of adoration; invoking the Grecian Nemesis? whose statue is, *on that account*, placed in the Capitol at Rome." (Idem, Lib. xxviii. 5.) "The skin of the forehead of the hyena is reckoned a defence against fascination." (Idem Lib. xxviii. 27) "I know not whose eye has fascinated my tender lambs." (Virg. Ec. iii. 103)

The Romans even had a god, Fascinus by name, who was not, however, as usual, the patron of the rogues whose name he bore; but—at least so I infer from his being called "custos infantum," the protector of children,—the defender of others against their power. (Plinii Nat. Hist. 28. 7)

I have not met with any examples of the mesmeric state being induced by passes after the present fashion, except one or two of doubtful interpretation, which therefore I shall not bring forward. The common method of mesmerising among the ancients seems to have been by means of music, and especially singing, hence called incantation and enchantment. I will adduce some specimens of it from the defence of Apuleius before a Roman judge on being accused of magic. The chief point of the accusation was, that, he was in the habit of what we should call mesmerising, or biologizing, a certain boy, and the evidence relied upon was, that, the boy was accustomed to *swoon* or *fall down* in his presence. After disposing of some minor points of the charge, which were plainly frivolous or incredible, he proceeds as follows: "They, therefore, (the accusers) fabricated a story consonant with common opinion and report, viz: that a certain boy, having been taken to a secret apartment, before a small altar and lamp,—no one being permitted to be present except a few who were in the plot,—was subjected to a magical incantation, (carmine cantatum) and that when he felt the influence of the charm, (ubi incantatus sit) he swooned away; (corruisse, went into a magnetic sleep,) that, afterwards, he was aroused from a state of unconsciousness. This is as far as they dared to go with the lie. But in order to make a whole story of it, they ought to have added that this same boy became possessed of a divining power, so as to foretell future events; for the object of such incantations is presage and divination. And this marvel in relation to boys is confirmed, not merely by vulgar opinion, but by the authority of learned men. For I remember to have read in Varro the philosopher, a man most accurately learned and erudite, *among other things of the same kind*, the following; that, some persons at Tralles, endeavoring to ascertain the event of the Mithridatic war by means of magical inquisition; a boy, looking intently upon the image of Mercury in water, chanted a hundred and sixty verses expressive of what was future. Also that Fabius, having lost five hundred denarii, went to consult Nigidius; that, boys, subjected by him to the influence of the magical chant, described the place where the purse with a part of the money was concealed, said that the remainder was spent, and that one denarius was in the possession of Marcus Cato the philosopher, which Cato confessed he had received from a footman as a contribution to the temple of Apollo. These, and other things, I have read, indeed, *in many authors,* concerning magical boys, but I am undecided in opinion whether I shall admit or deny the possibility of them. I believe, however, with Plato, that between gods and men in nature and in rank, there exist certain intermediate divine beings, and that divination and all magical miracles are under their control. I believe, moreover, that the human mind, and especially that of the child, which is pure, can, by the soothing power of song or of odors, be cast into a profound sleep and become oblivious of things present, and that, forgetting the body, it can, for a short time, be restored and return to its proper nature, that is, to an immortal and divine nature, and that so, veluti quodam sopore, it is enabled to presage the future. But, in order that these things may be so, it is requisite, as I understand, that a boy be selected of fair and unblemished form, of ingenuous and active mind and ready speech, so that, either the divine agent may lodge within as in a fit temple, *if indeed we may worthily suppose such an agent to be present in the body of the boy;* or else, the mind itself, being aroused, is suddenly restored to its inherent power of presage; which power is readily resumed, being immediately developed, when the mind is no longer weakened and obtunded by the oblivious influences of the body. But not from every wood, as Pythagoras says, should Mercury be carved." (Apuleius, de Magia, Oratio.) I desire to commend the contents of this curious extract to the especial consideration of the connoisseurs and participants, both embodied, and disembodied, of the present apocatastatic iteration of the like. What say you, ye boggling, clumsy, christian ghosts, spelling out your inanities letter by letter, rap by rap, or tip by tip; to the hundred and sixty verses, and good hexameters too, I dare say, and spoken, ore rotundo, pregnant with the fate of the mighty king of Pontus. How is it that you are, with now and then an exception, so inferior to your apocatastatic copy? Is Mercury dead with Pan, and all the old experienced oracle-utterers gone extinct? or have they gone to upper spheres, and given place to mere beginners? Consider the advice of Pythagoras, whether it might not be of service to you, for surely *your* Messengers are often made of very *soft* materials. And you, gentlemen Spiritists, especially you who *develop* and consecrate mediums, would it not be well for the new dispensation if you should follow a little more the ancient practice, and select handsome talented boys, whose souls dwell loosely in their clay, and can at any moment steal out and take a peep through time and space, and so become truly clairvoyant? or, if you prefer the other theory, be found a congruous receptacle, and well adapted instrument, for some supernal presence?—these, rather than stale maidens, Pythonesses, or unmaidens so enveloped in their mortal coil that they can find no egress, "immersed in matter," such matter too that none but an unclean spirit would choose to enter it. Consider too, gentlemen, the modest non-committalism of this ancient demibeliever in, and truly philosophic critic of, such phenomena. That there *are* spirits, and that there is a *spirit* in these cases, he believes with Plato, but whether the spirit goes out or comes in, on that point, he modestly declines to be dogmatic. Would not an unbiassed observer of our "modern instances"—with whatever humility and doubt he might dissent from your belief—lean strongly to the opinion that, at least in our own time, the spirit *goes out?*

It is obvious, from the above quotation, that the methods of divination there referred to, were sufficiently common among the Romans, though from the fact of their being accounted impious, and declared to be unlawful, they were of course less public than at present, and the authors who seem to have treated most fully of them have not come down to us. We can, however, I think, make out most of the details of the process by which the magnetic sleep was induced, and the desired responses to questions, or other communications, obtained. The author of the foregoing extract goes on to exculpate himself from the charge of magic, by showing that the boy, who was said to fall down in his presence, was subject to epileptic fits, that he was a coarse, stupid, vulgar, sickly child, not at all up to the Pythagorean definition of a Mercury; then addressing his accusers he says:—"A fine lad truly you have chosen for one to bring before the altar, on whose head to place ones hands (caput contingat) whom to robe in the pure pallium, from whom to expect responses!" (responsum speret!) It is, I think, implied in this last quotation, that the hands were also used in magnetising, as well as the voice, and probably the eyes at the same time. The following, then, cannot be far from a correct picture of an ancient sitting or circle, at least, where the method was by what they called incantation or enchantment. A dark and secret apartment, the smoking altar, the small pale lamp, the fuming incense diffusing Sabaean odors, the little cluster of earnest faces turned towards the handsome young Medium, who sits before the altar robed in the pure, white linen, pallium, sacred to religious rites,—in front of him the Magus, his hand upon the young man's head, his serpent eyes fixed on his face, his voice uttering the low wailing magic chant,—the boy sleeps,—he responds to the Sorcerer—he speaks hexameters,—he (or some Spirit in him) utters oracles! Such was one of the ancient methods of getting answers to curious questions.

But there were, besides those described by Apuleius, other methods of inducing the clairvoyant state, of putting the soul of the Medium *en rapport* with the distant or the future. The following is a specimen. "He (Isodorus) met with a consecrated woman (γυναικι ιερα, priestess ?) who possessed a supernatural endowment after a wonderful manner. For, having poured pure water into a glass vessel, she beheld in the water the phantasms (φασματα) of future events, and by means of the vision foretold with certainty what was about to take place. I have also myself, witnessed the same thing. (Ex Isodori Philosophi Vita, Damascio Auctore, apud Photium.)

There is nothing said here of incantation, as there is not in the case of the boy who responded in hexameters while looking at an image in water instead of into water itself; but that it was sometimes used in connexion with this fixing of the eyes, this staring process of abstraction, is shown by the next quotation. It shows also that these—at that time—illicit practices had found their way into very respectable society. The questioner here is a Roman Emperor, very desirous to ascertain whether he was to continue to sport the imperial purple which he had honestly bought with his money, or whether he was about to exchange it for a "stone coat." "Julian was guilty of the folly of consulting the Magicians &c.— They immolated certain victims not consonant with the customs of Roman sacrifice, and chanted profane incantations; also those things which are said to be done at the mirror, in which boys, their eyes being blindfolded, are said to see with the top of the head by means of incantations uttered over it, (incantato vertice) Julian had recourse to; whereupon the boy is said to have beheld the approach of Severus, and the death of Julian." (Spartian. Vita. Jul. Did.)

There is some obscurity in regard to the exact process here, but I think the supposition may have been that the boy was to direct his eyes, at least mentally, as if to gaze into the mirror through the top of his head, for he is said to look into, or look back (respicere) into, the mirror at the top of his head.

Let us, next, look at a few specimens of self-magnetization, or spontaneous clairvoyance. The most celebrated, and indeed, world-renowned, manifestations of this kind made their appearance in certain prescient females, called Sibyls, at various times, and in various places, of the ancient heathen world. They are said to have written their oracles (χρησμοι) upon the leaves of trees as the spirit of divination came upon them. If so, one of them at least, must have thought hers worth copying, for the historian relates that she offered them for sale to the Romans in nine *books*, (βιβλους εννεα) and when they thought the price too high she burned three and still demanded the same price for the six; being still refused she burned three more and demanded still the same price for the remaining three,—she was evidently good at a bargain, if not at vaticination,—they were now purchased, and found, or supposed, to have such important relations to the future destinies of Rome, that they were preserved, *with more care than any other sacred deposit*, says the historian. Ten distinguished citizens were set apart, exempt from military and civil duties, for the purpose of taking care of them, without whom they could never be seen, being preserved in a stone coffer, under ground, (κατα γης) in the temple of the Capitolian Jupiter. They were always consulted in important deliberations of the senate, and whenever danger from without or from within threatened the State. (Dionyss. Halicarnass. L. iv. 62) These genuine Sibylline χρησμοι were destroyed,— fatal omen ! when the Capitol was burned in Sylla's time, just at the commencement of that "sterile period" ushered in by the "mournful sound of the trumpet :"—a period, like our own, and all other sterile periods, doomed to subsist on make-believes, and all sorts of supposititions, and illegitimacies. The degenerate, and degenerating Romans, therefore, instead of rousing themselves to carve their own future destiny, sent ambassadors to various parts of Europe and Asia, to ask leave to copy, for the Roman People, whatever Sibylline fragments— for the most part, not true Sibyllina, but old wives **fables, and other witch-droppings**—they might find there.

These it was that the Medium-led statesmen, of the remaining days of the Republic, consulted, quarreled over, forged, interpreted, and mis-interpreted, each to his own purpose, precisely as our old women do the Constitution ; and precisely as miscalled American statesmen will, nay *do*, proh pudor, et nefas apocatastaticum ! ! *"consult the spirits,"* in the American Capitol.

However, it is plain from the record and the conduct of men, that there were in those days clairvoyant women who could see with the top of the head, or in some other anomolous way, or at least,—which is sufficient for my present purpose,—that people, at that time, supposed they had sufficient reason to think so.

But this endowment was not peculiar to women, men also not unfrequently exhibited the same. The following are from "The Life" of that ancient Swedenborg, or Davis, Apollonius Tyanensis. He was on a visit to the Sages of India for the purpose of perfecting himself in philosophy and theurgy, not yet, it seems, "fully developed," magnetically. Having made known his purpose, the Superior of the philosophic fraternity said to him : " It is the custom of others to inquire of those who visit them, who they are, and for what purpose they come ; but with us the first evidence of wisdom is that we are not ignorant of those who come to us. So saying he gave account both of the paternal and maternal families of Apollonius,—of all he did at Aegae,—how Damis came to him,—of their conversation on the journey, and of what they heard from others. All this he related readily and fluently as if he had himself been a companion of the journey. Apollonius being astonished and inquiring how he obtained such knowledge ? (such power of knowing) you also, said he, possess the same endowment but not yet in perfection." (Philostrat. Vita Apollonii Tyanensis L. iii. C. 16.) His psychometric faculty enabled him to see that Apollonius was capable of "becoming a good Medium." Accordingly, we find him, after his return from India,—the Brahmins probably mesmerised him a few times—quite well "developed." For discoursing one day at Ephesus in a grove near the city, a flock of birds was observed sitting quietly upon a tree—shortly there arrived another bird emitting a peculiar note, whereupon the whole flock set up a cry and flew away. The auditors noticing and wondering at the conduct of the birds; Apollonius interrupted his discourse and said, that, "a boy—near a gate of the city, which he named,—carrying a vessel of grain, had fallen down and spilled it, and having left much of it on the ground was gone away;—that the bird, happening to be near, and observing this, had come to inform his companions that they might partake of his good fortune. Many of the company thereupon hastened to satisfy themselves of the truth of the statement,—Apollonius, meantime, going on with his discourse. Soon they returned shouting, and filled with admiration &c." (Idem L. iv. 3) The next specimen is instructive, especially to the faculty; but as I have promised to be brief, I must abbreviate it somewhat. Apollonius being at Tarsus, a young man was brought to him,—for he was a healing medium as well as a clairvoyant,—who, thirty days before, had been bitten by a mad dog. He commanded the dog to be brought to him. But, as the accident had occurred when the boy was out of the city, none of those about him had seen the dog, and he himself had not observed him so as to be able to describe or distinguish him. Thereupon Apollonius, retracting himself, withdrawing himself inwards, (ἐπισχων, stopping the outer machinery and taking on the interior state,) " O, Damis, said he, the dog is white, shaggy, large, and resembles the Amphilochian breed. He stands trembling near a certain fountain, (*naming the fountain*) very desirous, and at the same time afraid, to drink. Bring him hither to me, saying to him only that it is I who summons him. Being conducted to him, accordingly, by Damis, the dog threw himself at the feet of Apollonius, whining, (or weeping, κλαιων) Apollonius patted and soothed him, and bringing him to the boy he commanded him to lick the bite, in order that the remedy might be the *same thing* as that which had produced the disease." (Idem L. vi. 43) O, Hahneman! Great Itch-Compeller! Solomon was right! and your honors are also in danger, for yours, it is plain is, after all, only an apocatastatic homœopathy! One specimen more,—out of a great number recorded in his Life,—of the clairvoyant powers of this capital old Medium is all my limits will permit. He was again at Ephesus discoursing near the city, when hesitating, and then ceasing to speak, as when one forgets what he was going to say next; he looked fiercely upon the ground, strode forwards three or four steps, and, "strike the tyrant! strike!" he exclaimed. And when all Ephesus, (most of the citizens being present) was astonished at his conduct;—courage, my friends, said he, for this very day the tyrant is slain, this day, did I say, nay, at the very moment that I stopped speaking. Soon as there was time for the news to arrive it was found, accordingly, that just at that hour, Domitian was assassinated at Rome. (Idem, L. viii. C. 26.)

I must not omit to insert here another example of clairvoyance from the life of our friend Iamblichus, just to show that he also was an Adept in the occult sciences, or an Expert, as the lawyers say, for we shall have to call him upon the stand as a witness in that character bye and bye. "Iamblichus went with his disciples to sacrifice, in one of the suburbs of the city; and after the sacrifice was performed they returned to town, gently walking along, and discoursing concerning the gods, as a subject very proper for the occasion. Then Iamblichus, who was perfectly lost in thought in the midst of the discourse, whose voice was fallen, and *eyes immovably fixed on the earth*, turned to his companions and exclaimed: " Let us take another road, for not far from hence is a funeral procession." Iamblichus, accordingly, chose a purer way, and was accompanied by a few of his disciples; the rest, doubting, went forward and met the procession, &c." (Eunapii Vita Iamblichi.) It would be easy to add the record of many more similar manifestations from the *fabulous* lives of still more ancient sages as Pythagoras, Orpheus, &c., but as these are suspicious, for more reasons than one, and as I propose to deal only with veritable and well attested facts, I shall pass them by.

But these are, as it were, mere amateur performances, the private and illicit doings of unconsecrated and profane people, intrusively attempting the functions which properly appertained to others. The public religion sought to keep such things under its own control. All legal Mediums were consecrated and religiously set apart to their office. Among these, by far the most celebrated, and most frequently consulted, was the priestess of Apollo at Delphi, or as she was often called, the Pythia, and sometimes Pythoness. The theory was that Apollo spoke through her voice. But it is obvious that, in so far as she possessed any powers of privesion or clairvoyance, they originated in the same way as in the case of the enchanted boys; that is, the induction of the magnetic, or trance state, was an indispensable condition of their development; and this state was induced by essentially the same means. When she was about to give oracular responses she entered a cave in the mountain over which the Delphic Temple was built,—she was placed in the basket or basket-shaped seat of the sacred tripod, which, being open at the bottom, stood over a rent or crevice in the rock from which issued a mephitic vapor,—she drank of the inspiring water of the Castalian Spring—she was enclosed with branches of laurel whose leaves she chewed—before her was the altar of the God —the air was loaded with the fumes and fragrance of burning incense—the music of trumpets and other instruments resounded through the cavern,—around her stood the priests and other servants of Apollo, and those to whom the response was to be given,—she became unconscious, went into the magnetic state, (hence the phrase ἐν ὅλμῳ κοιμᾶσθαι, to sleep in the hollow of the tripod, signified to prophesy,)—but soon the god himself, duly invoked, arrived, and took possession and control of the organs of the Pythia—she was now inspired with a "divine fury or rage," she became agitated, convulsed, tore her hair, foamed at the mouth, until at length the excitement found vent in the utterance of pure Greek hexameters, which contained or constituted the oracular responses to the questions proposed, which were enclosed in sealed envelopes and known only to the questioner. At least, in the more ancient periods, the responses were always in hexameter verses, but afterwards in prose ; which fact caused no little trouble to the believers in plenary inspiration, and who held that the spirit "came in" instead of going out ;—for why should the god of music and poetry forget how to make verses ? However, we shall see bye and bye that they had a way of accounting for it. Here is evidence of clairvoyance, at least, and on a pretty large scale, if we consider the extent of Apollo's correspondence, the number of letters from all parts of the world which were answered without opening them. As to the correctness of the answers, and their coincidence with events, though it must be confessed that they were sometimes a little equivocal, Cicero says (De Divinatione Lib. i. xviii) that Chrysippus collected *innumerable oracles* the truth of every one of which was confirmed by most abundant testimony. A specimen or two must suffice ; and lest some infidel sceptic should suspect that the seals of some of those envelopes were in the habit of being tampered with, I will select those which shall put all his doubts to shame, and to flight. Listen to the father of history. "Crœsus, king of Lydia, wishing to test the powers of the Pythia, sent messengers to Delphi with directions to inquire, *on a certain day,* what the king of the Lydians was doing. * * * * * * * No sooner had the Lydians entered the temple to consult the god, and to ask the question commanded, than the Pythia uttered the following in hexameter verses :

" I know the number of the sands, and the measure of the sea ; I know what the dumb would say, I hear him who speaks not. There comes to me the odor of tortoise and lamb's flesh seething together in a brass vessel ; beneath the flesh is brass, there is also brass above." This oracle being recorded, the messengers returned to Sardis. Crœsus read and was satisfied. * * * * For after he had sent the messengers to consult the oracle, *on the appointed day,* he hit upon the following to be done, as something which he supposed might be difficult to detect and describe :—cutting up a tortoise and a lamb, he boiled them together in a brazen vessel which also had a cover of brass." (Herodotus, Clio.) The Pythia must have been, in this case, extremely clairvoyant, or else have had excessively acute olfactories, have been clairolfacient.

When the Gauls under Brennus were, apparently, about to destroy the Temple at Delphi, the god being consulted, the Pythia answered from the Oracle : " *I, and the white virgins will see to that matter.*" Whereupon the Gauls, being seized with a panic in a snow-storm among the mountains, fled or perished in the snow. (Cicero de Divinatione Lib. i. 37) This is a very unexceptionable example of the combination of prescience with clairvoyance, for which the Pythia was famed, beyond all her compeers.

The following is a specimen of equivoque, or *double entendre,* like the still more famous response to Crœsus ; who, when inquiring if he should be successful against the Persians was told, that, if he crossed the Halys, he should destroy a great kingdom. " When however, on consulting Apollo at Delphi, he was advised to beware of the seventy-third year, supposing he was to live until that period, and not thinking of the age of Galba, he was filled with confidence &c." (Suetonius Vita Neronis c. 40) Crœsus, by crossing the river, destroyed his own kingdom ; and Nero, instead of living to his seventy third year, was destroyed by Galba who was seventy-three years of age. The celebrated response to Pyrrhus, "Aio te, Aeacida, Romanos vincere posse" was another of the same sort. The poor Pythia has, I think, been ridiculed without reason, and her credit very unjustly impeached on account of these and such-like utterances. For, it is manifest, that the double meaning in such cases is an essential condition of the truth of the prediction, otherwise the prophecy would defeat its own fulfilment and so prove false. Such cases, therefore, instead of discrediting, ought to confirm the clairvoyant character of the prophetess,—it was her business to *see* the future, not to change it.

The Pythia, however, though first in rank, possessed no *peculiar* powers, but was only one among innumerable others, in the service of the ancient religions, who, in various ways, evinced the possession of the same. "The religion of this temple (that of the Deus Heliopolitanus in Syria) excels in divination. The absent consult this God by sending sealed letters; and answers are given, in order, to their contents. Thus the Emperor Trajan, being about to enter Parthia from this province, and being desired by his friends to inquire in regard to the event of the undertaking, excercised Roman prudence by first testing the powers of the Oracle, lest he might be imposed upon. First, therefore, he sent sealed letters to which he desired a reply in writing. The God commanded paper to be brought, sealed *blank*, and sent; the priests being astonished at that sort of reply, because they were *ignorant of the character of the* (Trajan's) *letter*s. Trajan received the answer with great admiration because he also had sent blank tablets to the God. He then sent other sealed letters inquiring whether he should return to Rome after finishing the war. The god directed a vine to be cut in pieces, wrapt in linen, and carried to him, signifying, as the event proved, that his bones were to be carried back to Rome." (Macrobius Saturnal. L. i. c. 23.)

Such specimens of divination are found scattered throughout ancient history, besides "innumerable" instances of it, which, according to Cicero and Apuleius, were recorded but have not come down to us; but these examples are perhaps sufficient (I have promised to be brief) to prove the existence, and illustrate the character, of the ancient clairvoyance, at least as manifested by oral communications. I shall have occasion to bring forward other forms of it under a different head.

The following quotation, from one well acquainted with the subject, shows pretty conclusively, the identity of the influence which affected these vaticinating people with the present animal magnetism, or Mesmerism, or spirit-influence. "I wish to point out to you the signs by which those who are rightly possessed by the gods may be known.— * * * they neither energize according to sense, nor are in such a vigilant state as those who have their senses excited from sleep; nor are they moved as those who energize according to impulse. Nor again are they conscious of the state they are in, neither as they were before, nor in any other way; nor, in short, do they exert any knowlege, which is peculiarly their own. The greatest indication, however, of the truth of this is the following: Many, through divine inspiration, are not burned when fire is introduced to them, the inspiring influence preventing the fire from touching them. Many also, though burned, do not apprehend that they are so, because they do not then live an animal life. And some, indeed, though transfixed with spits do not perceive it; but others that are struck on the shoulders with axes, and others that have their arms cut with knives, are by no means conscious of what is done to them. From these things it is demonstrated that those who energize enthusiastically are not conscious of the state they are in, and that they neither live a human, nor an animal, life, according to sense or impulse, but that they exchange this for a certain more divine life, by which they are inspired and perfectly possessed." (Iamblichus de Mysteriis.)

I had intended to exhibit manifestations parallel to those contained in this chapter, from the writings of the spiritists of the present time; but the parallelism here, in all essential particulars, is so obvious to all who have even but the most superficial acquaintance with the subject, that I shall save myself the trouble of transcribing, and the reader that of perusing, what must be already abundantly familiar to him. The fascination by the eye is what any one may witness, and most have often witnessed, at biological lectures and other such-like exhibitions, or at the " Circles ;"—to be fatally fascinated by praise is a thing not at all rare in the present times, though I must confess, that I am not personally cognizant of any instance in which trees have been made to wither and die from that cause alone,—*there* is a point in the ancient magic which is not yet, I think, re-developed—the enchanted boys are only specimens of magnetisation by a different method, although indeed, the chant is still sometimes used for that purpose;— the Pythia was merely a good Medium ;—such cases as those of Apollonius and others are not uncommon, even since Swedenborg,—and Sibyls we have in every village. Of the aqua-clairvoyance I shall have more to say in another chapter.

CHAPTER VI.

Qui rore puro *Castaliae* lavit
Crines solutos, * * * * * Apollo.
Horat. Carmin. L. iii. v. 62.

Who bathes his flowing hair in pure
Castalian dew?—Apollo.

Let us next examine some other facts of the ancient Spiritism, of a somewhat different character, and see whether they also are sufficiently analogous to those of the present Spiritism to prove their apocatastatical relation to each other. The first quotation which I shall bring forward, I desire to make use of for a double purpose, viz: as a specimen of spirit-writing, and of that quality of certain ancient waters, which confered the power of divination, and induced the clairvoyant state, a quality, in this respect, precisely like that of magnetized water in our time. The ancient spirits, so far as I have hitherto ascertained, were not accustomed to make use of the Medium's hand for writing communications, except in the case of the poet, who was supposed to be the writing-medium and amanuensis of the Muses; and with one other remarkable exception viz: that of the Sibyls. These ladies were a sort of female hermits, who lived in forests, mountains, and caves, in various places and countries, and gave responses in writing to those who consulted them, just as Mrs C—— at B—— Mrs S—— at M—— and so many others at other places, do at present. They seem to have written too, when not consulted; for the good of posterity or whomsoever it might concern, whenever the spirit took them by the arm; so that they were obliged to write upon the leaves of trees or whatever came to hand. These χρησμοι have, unfortunately, all, or nearly all, perished; although we have plenty of counterfeits; their great value and authority in ancient times leading to very extensive forgeries of them.

In other instances, the spirits who had acquired power to control the Medium's muscles, commonly took the tongue instead of the hand, and so, instead of going through the present tedious process of training and development, from rapping to writing, and from writing to speaking, they saved time, and made speaking Mediums at once. The specimens of spirit-writing which I have found seem to have been a sort of acheiropoietic productions, or perhaps they were written by the *"condensed"* hand of the airy and tenuous spirit-vehicle, or ειδωλον, which spirits, anciently, as well as now, made use of for locomotion and other purposes. Even this kind of writing seems not to have been common in the former period, and it is, so far as I know, in the present, among the rarest of spirit-manifestatioms. In regard to the "aquæ fatidicæ," as they were called, of which the Castalian fountain at Delphi was quite the most famous, from the drinking of which the Pythia obtained in part her clairvoyant powers, and perhaps Apollo himself, to whom the fountain was sacred, and who, it seems, was in the habit of bathing his head in it, probably when he wished to excite the vaticinating mood, or he might have used it to cool his brain as Byron did,—and which waters were found also in many other places; the most probable explanation of their peculiar quality, and one strictly analogical, reasoning from the present to the past, is, to suppose that the spirit who spoke through the drinking Medium, or rather, that the "genius loci," if he were, or were not, the communicating spirit, magnetised the water on every occasion of its use for the purpose of divination, or, the latter personage may have indulged a personal pride in keeping it at *all times* magnetised, for the use, whether of men, or of gods. In the same way we may perhaps best explain the instances of water-divination in the preceding chapter, that is, by supposing the water to have been magnetized by some spirit, or somebody else. The following is the promised quotation. "It is supposed by those who have examined the subject, that, the water in this place (Daphne, in Syria,) comes from the Castalian fountain, which confers the faculty of divination; having the same name, and the same qualities, as that at Delphi. They boast that Hadrian, while yet a private man, received intimations here concerning the empire. For, they say, that having dipt a leaf of laurel in the spring, he found, on taking it out, a prediction of the future plainly written thereon."— (Sozomen Lib. v.)

That this was no mere boast of those concerned for the credit of the spring is proved by the fact related by several other historians, that, on coming to the empire, Hadrian walled in, and shut up, this spring, lest it should teach others how to become emperors; and that it remained closed until Julian's time. Perhaps other emperors as well as Hadrian were afraid of it. This spring was perhaps the only one, among the divining waters, which had the faculty of expressing itself in writing; but the same kind of spirit-writing was often found inscribed upon rocks and walls, (Nicephorus Gregoras Hist. Lib. v.) the spirits being able in those days to communicate without a Medium, as they are beginning to do in these.

But we must consider a few more instances of the curious, and marvelous, not to say miraculous, effects of the ancient divining waters. And would it not be well that our own springs should be carefully examined, with a view to ascertain whether they do not, some of them, possess analogous powers? Or if not, perhaps some benevolent spirits may consent to take charge, and preside, each over his own fountain, and become the genius loci, and impart to the waters the same powers as did their apocatastatic brethren. We have, in modern times, plenty of healing waters for diseases of the *body*, many of them too, presided over by spirits, or, at least, they were so not long since, why may we not have, for the benefit of the *soul?* a series of good theological waters, judiciously and conveniently located!!—what could tend more to a healthful and true "progress." This too, will be evolved, as sure as ours is apocatastatic of the period we have supposed. Our business, however, at present, is with the *ancient* fountains.

"It is well known that the Oracle at Colophon gives responses by means of water. For there is a fountain in a subterranean cavern from which the prophet drinks. Then, having, on the prescribed nights, performed the accustomed ceremonies, he utters responses, *having become invisible to the spectators present!* (ουκ ετ' ὁρωμενον τοις παρουσι θεωρῖς)—Hence it is is manifest that this water confers a divining power." (Iamblichus de Mysteriis.)

This fountain at Colophon must have been a very wonderful fountain, more so if possible than that which had the power to write on laurel leaves. It not only magnetized the prophet who drank of it, so as to make him clairvoyant, but it enabled him to magnetise the eyes of all the persons present at his sittings—for such, I take it, must be the explanation of the fact of his becoming invisible to them. This is a power not yet, so far as I know, attained by any modern Medium. The spirits often magnetise the eyes of the Medium so as to render the spectators invisible to *him*, and the biologists take away the power of vision from the eyes of those whom they can *fascinate*, but to fascinate a whole audience is, I believe, hitherto beyond the magnetic battery of even the Rev. Le Roy

Sunderland. That same Colophonian water must have been equal to the ring of Gyges, and if the fountain is not dry, its re-discovery would be worth more to the finder than all the gold of California. However, let me not tempt any man of Connecticut, or of New-Hampshire, to go in quest of it, since it might, after all, prove a losing speculation; for its powers and properties are not, probably, inherent in the water itself, —it might not therefore bear transportation,—but are confered by the resident and presiding spirit at his pleasure. Such things are all "the work of the spirits." This is evident from the following remarkable quotation:—

"The prophetess in Branchidæ, whether she hold in her hand a wand anciently the gift of some god, and becomes filled with a divine light; whether, sitting upon an axle, she foretells future events; whether, dipping her feet or the hem of her garment (κρασπεδον) in water; or whether, enveloped in the vapor of water, she receives the divine influence;—by all these methods prepared, *she receives the god from without.* This is also apparent from the number of sacrifices, from the whole of the prescribed ritual, and whatever else is done before the access of the oracular inspiration, the baths of the prophetess, her fasting three whole days, her remaining in the adytum, *her becoming already encircled with light,* and rejoicing for some time;—for all these things demonstrate *that the god is invoked to approach,* that he *comes from without,* that the prophetess is inspired in a wonderful manner before she comes to her accustomed place; (before she opens the sitting) and it is made manifest, that, in the spirit which rises from the fountain, (besides the natural quality of the water) there is another superior (πρεσβυτερον) god, who is separate from the place, and who is the cause of the place, and the country, and of the whole divination." (Idem Ibidem.) Here is a most unhesitating believer in the spirits; a man too who beyond all others made it the business of his life to investigate the mysteries of spirit-intercourse; and to observe and mark in a scientific manner,—beyond all modern competition, (unless the Judge may approach him)—the attendant phenomena, whether physiological, psychical, or physical. *Such* investigators in the present period are also apt to become confirmed believers.

The reader will please to notice also in passing, the beautiful specimen of odic light exhibited by this Medium, the grand display of that sort of lurid lights being reserved for the chapter on physical manifestations.—These waters, then, were not the *cause* of the strange manifestations which accompanied the due ritual use of them, but only an occasion, or, *means*, without which the spirit could not, or did not choose to, produce them. It would be unphilosophical however, irreligious rather, to suppose their employment to be wholly arbitrary. Perhaps their use was symbolical; their transparency imparting, by some sympathetic action, the same quality to the otherwise turbid and opake future, and their purity suggesting truth in the communications, of which the light which invested the Medium was, as it were, the shadow and assurance.

But we must return for a moment to the fountain at Colophon, which had other note-worthy properties, besides the power of rendering people invisible. "There is not a woman here as at Delphi, but a priest is elected from certain families, and mostly from Miletus, who is *informed only of the name and number of those who come to consult the Oracle.* He then retires into the cavern, and drinking of the secret fountain,—though ignorant generally (plerumque) of letters and poetry,—he delivers responses, in verse, *to whatever mental questions any one has in his mind.* (super rebus quas quis mente concepit.)—(Tacitus, Annal. Lib. ii.) Here is what we may call, in modern phrase, "a well developed Medium;" the power of answering mental questions being a test and proof of it, this being, as I understand, one of the highest functions of the office. Altogether, a sitting of this Medium must have been a very *spirital* affair, the medium himself being changed into a spirit, or, however, there was nothing left for the senses but his voice, vox and preterea nihil; and then, spirit-like, to read ones very thoughts!! I know not whether modern developments have *yet* reached so wholly *spirital* a form of exhibition! This faculty of clairvoyance in relation to the thoughts of others, however, was not peculiar to this Medium, the Pythia expressly laid claim to it,—"I know what the dumb would say, I hear the voice of him who speaks not,"—and often manifested it. It was frequently implied also in the manifestations of other ancient mediums.

There was another form in which the ancient clairvoyance sometimes expressed itself, not without imitation, it is said, in the present period. The following is an example of it.

"Then was performed a great miracle. For Mus, as is related by the Thebans, having visited various oracles, came to the temple of Apollo Ptoi. There followed him three men publicly selected by the Thebans, for the purpose of recording the responses which might be given. But, on arriving at the temple, they were astonished to hear the priestess answer in some foreign language, instead of speaking Greek, so that they had nothing to do. Whereupon Mus, taking from them their tablets, wrote down the responses of the Oracle—it was said in the Carian tongue,—and having made the record he departed &c." (Herodotus, Urania.)

The sages of India also, as appears from the Life of Apollonius, seem to have possessed this power of speaking the language of those whom they addressed. It was also one of the accomplishments of Apollonius himself. (Vita Apollon. Lib. i. c. 19) Was the *rapport magnetique* existing between the person speaking and the person spoken to? was it the δαιμων, or guardian angel, of the speaker who happened to be a linguist? or is the opinion of Apollonius the true one, who explained such facts in his own case, and especially all instances of clairvoyance by water, like those we have been considering, as the effect of the Pythagorean diet— that is, of water drinking, and non-carniverous food; beans also being excluded. (Vita Apollon. Lib. ii. c. 37) He was, however, something of a spiritist, perhaps as much so as Iamblichus, and intimates that by such means the god is induced to "enter from without."

Besides the developed Mediums through whom the spirits could communicate with a third person, there were also in ancient times what are now called impressible Mediums, who received the divine influx into their own consciousness, or semi-consciousness, but it was not fully transmitted for the benefit of others. These, as might be expected, are to be found mostly among the later, or the new, mystical, Platonists. "For the end and scope with him consisted in approximating, and being united to, the god who is above all things. But he four times obtained this end while I was with him, and this by an ineffable energy and not in capacity. * * * * * * by employing for this purpose the paths narrated by Plato in the Banquet, the supreme divinity appeared to him, who has neither any form nor idea, but is established above intellect and every intelligible; to whom also I, Porphyry, say that I once approached, and was united, when I was sixty-eight years of age." (Porphyr. Vita Plotin.)

The mesmeric insensibility was also one of the ancient phenomena; though I am not aware that it was, at that time, ever induced for the purpose of avoiding the pain of surgical operations. Sufficient evidence that ancient nerves were not different from the present, has perhaps been given already in the extract from Iamblichus, and parallel facts are common everywhere among those "who energize enthusiastically." I will however, make one quotation.

"Under Mount Soracte is the town of Feronia, which is also the name of the goddess of the place, who is held in great honor there. There is also a grove of Feronia, in which are performed sacred rites of a very wonderful kind. For those possessed by this Dæmon (οἱ κατεχομενοι υπο της δαιμονος ταυτης) walk with naked feet over burning coals, and hot ashes, without suffering any injurious effects from the fire." (Strabo. Lib. v.)

CHAPTER VII.

Evocantes animas dæmonum, eas indiderunt imaginibus sanctis divinisque mysteriis, par quas idola et bene faciendi et male vires habere potuissent.—
Hermes Trismegistus, in Asclepian Dialogue.

Evoking the souls of dæmons, they caused them to enter into images by means of sacred and mysterious rites, and through the presence of these spirits the Idols were enabled to exhibit manifestations both good and evil.

φανταζει δε πολλακις, (δια γοητειας) και πυρος ουρανιου ενδοσεις, και διαμειδιωσι επι τουτων αγαλματα, πυρι δε αυτοματω λαμπαδες αναπτονται.
Psellus, de Dæmonibus.

Often too, celestial fire is made to appear through magic, and then statues laugh, and lamps are spontaneously enkindled.

* * * * * void of light
Save what the glimmering of these livid flames
Casts pale and dreadful.   PARADISE LOST, L. i.

The ancients were much more scientific than we in their methods of spirit-intercourse. They had examined the subject much more profoundly. Their theoretical views were more consistent, and mature, and relied upon with more confidence than ours. Minds of the highest order were devoted to the investigation of the subject. And then, what is very essential to success, both in faith and practice, they went about it much more religiously than we. It was a sacred theurgy practiced by consecrated and holy men as a part of religion. And even the unlicensed, and outsiders, when they presumed to call spirits from the vasty deep; or, through the eyes, or top of the head of some enchanted boy, or water-magnetised woman, dared to peep into the otherwise invisible world, they felt as if they were sacrilegiously tresspassing on hallowed ground, and quieted their consciences, and at the same time honored and placated the spirits, by the due performance of sacred rites. Sometimes, however, the spirits, instead of being solicited, were commanded to speak, and then, especially if the purpose of the questioner were unlawful, the rites were impious, with dire chanted imprecations, choric dances, and accursed spells, not even excepting human sacrifices, or the utterance of words or names of such mystic and mighty power as to compel the gods themselves. Yet even these were reckoned *religious* ceremonies. The ancients, "religiosissimi homines," if they had wished a table to tip them answers to questions, mental or vocal, instead of laying their hands upon it, would first have dedicated it to the numen, or spirit, from whom they expected the response, and consecrated it with sacrifice, and incense, and chaplet, and unction, and libation, and lighted tapers, and then with dance, and chanted invocation, have invited the spirit to enter. But the ancients did not use tables, those profane inmates of the kitchen, for any such hallowed purpose. Statues, images, simulacra, wrought with the utmost skill, and those "not of every wood," were reckoned more appropriate for such purposes. And even such a simulacrum was only a dead inanimate block, until, with all due and solemn rites, the spirit, whose residence it was to become, and who was to act and answer in and by it, had been successfully invoked, instated, and inthroned within it. Having thus prepared "a piece of wood," as that old puritan, Isaiah, sneeringly calls it, they had something that could tip, and nod, and march, and float thro' the air, and speak besides, if occasion required. Sometimes, however, they made use of other objects for purposes of divination and consulting the spirits, as the tripod of the Pythia, for instance, and then such objects had to be consecrated in due form.

The following example of the method of constructing, consecrating, and using, what may be called a divining machine, is quite a curiosity in itself, and interesting from its similarity in several particulars, to some of the present methods. I would commend it to the favorable notice and consideration of modern spirits, especially of those beginners who are obliged to *spell out* their responses. It is really a scientific and very elegant method of using the alphabet for that purpose, and much more convenient, than going, as it were, fishing among the whole twenty-four letters in search of each one as it is needed, after the present clumsy fashion. It was quite an artistic, and gentleman-like, dactylomancy, altogether superior to any use of the ring in our time, as well as to our pinacomancy, or the typtomancy, which makes a similar use of the alphabet. The occasion of its employment in the instance which brought it under the notice of history was as follows. Certain political gentlemen, in the time of the Emperor Valens, being incautiously curious to know who was to be the next emperor, made inquiry of the spirits. The Roman police, however, who managed to be informed of many things without the aid of the spirits, were of opinion that they were asking improper questions. Whereupon the inquisitive gentlemen, suddenly found themselves arraigned for high treason. On their trial, one of the operators, described to the judges the machine, which had been brought into court, and their way of consulting the spirits by it, as follows :

"This ill-omened little table, which you see before you, most noble judges, we constructed of laurel twigs, with unlucky auspices, so as to resemble in form the Delphic tripod ; and having consecrated it with mystic, chanted, imprecations, and with much, and long continued, dancing in a ring round about it, at length we got it in operation. The method of working it, whenever it was consulted concerning hidden things, was on this wise. It was placed in the midst of an apartment, which was made pure by Arabian odors ; a circular plate composed of different metals being simply laid upon it, upon the extreme margin of whose circumference were skilfully engraved the scriptile forms of the twenty-four letters of the alphabet, separated from each other by accurately measured spaces. Over this, robed in linen vestments, having on his feet sandals of the same material, the torulus wound about his head, and holding in his hand the boughs of a tree of good omen,—the spirit from whom the prescient response was expected having been propitiated by appropriate chants,—stood one skilled in ritual science; holding suspended a small ring composed of finest Carpathian thread, and wrought with mystic rites, which, falling at regular intervals upon single letters, composed heroic verses conformable to the questions asked, and complete in mode and measure, like those which proceed from the Pythia, or from the Oracle at Branchidæ."—(Ammianus, L. xxix, 29.)

Now, any spirit who can compress his vehicle so as to produce any physical manifestation whatever, could, one would suppose, cause such a ring, *suspended from the ceiling of the room*, to vibrate in the required direction, as the spirit did in this case; and certainly, with much more ease than they can tip tables, or even rap upon them. What say you my "tricksy spirits" to such an experiment, with the ring? And here I desire the Commissioner of Patents to take notice that all modern "Celestial Telegraphs," "Psychographs," and such like recent contrivances, are mere apocatastatic copies, and not patentable at all, as I understand the law,—I therefore enter my "caveat," not that I wish to apply for a patent, but, "suum cuique" let justice be done; anciently, as now, "some things could be done as well as others."

But it is time to proceed to the ancient manifestations by means of consecrated effigies, or simulacra.

" The image of the god (Jupiter Ammon) is composed of emeralds and other precious stones, and gives oracles in a way quite peculiar. It is borne about in a golden ship by eighty priests; who, bearing it upon their shoulders, go whithersoever the god (image) *by nodding his head*, directs them."—

(Diodor. Sicul. Lib. 17) This is not much, even though Jupiter did it. About equivalent to tipping a light-stand, or moving some other small furniture.

"From Byblos I ascended Libanus a days journey, having heard that there was an ancient temple of Venus there. * * * * * * * In it are many precious, and many wonderful, things. For the statues *sweat, move,* and *give oracles.* And often, when the temple is shut, a *cry originates within* (βοη ἐγενετο) which has been heard by many."—(Lucian. de Syria Dea.)

These are physical manifestations equal to table-moving, and required, probably, spirits of about the same stregth, except that the ancient spirits being more at home in their effigies, which were a sort of earthly bodies for them, and conformed at least in some measure, to them, could act in and by them with more convenience and ease, than a modern spirit can get into a table and cause it to move. The ability to produce sounds and other physical manifestations is also perhaps greater, in places consecrated to the spirits, than elsewhere. At least, such manifestations in modern spirit-temples, as for instance, the thunder in Broadway, the blowing of the trumpet at Athens, Ohio, &c., are thus accounted for. (See Spiritual Telegraph Nov. 19, 1853.)

"A little before the misfortune of the Lacedæmonians at Leuctra, there was heard the clashing of arms in the temple of Hercules, and the statue of Hercules sweat profusely. At Thebes, at the same time, in the temple of Hercules, the folding doors, which were fastened with bolts, suddenly opened of themselves, and the arms which were hung upon the walls were found thrown upon the ground. There were other signs preceding this calamity. The statue of Lysander at Delphi, which the Lacedæmonians had placed there after his great naval victory over the Athenians, appeared crowned with weeds and bitter herbs, and the two golden stars which had been suspended there as offerings in honor of Castor and Pollux who had assisted them *visibly* in that battle, fell, and disappeared." (Cicero, de Divinatione i. 94) These spirits might almost have done such things as the Judge describes, if they had not thought them in bad taste.

But the ancient spirits were quite up to the modern in physical manifestations every way, as we shall see as we proceed.

"There was, at Antioch, an image of Jupiter Amicalis, so compounded by magic arts, and consecrated by unhallowed rites, that it mocked the eyes of those who looked upon it, (ut falleret oculos intuentium, became invisible?) and seemed to exhibit various portentous appearances, and to give responses. The truth of this was made manifest to all men, and even to the emperors themselves." (Ruffinus) This art of making ones self invisible is one I should be happy to learn of the spirits, but I am not aware that any Mediums, or tables, in our times, are accustomed to render themselves invisible to non-magnetized, or non-spirited people.

"There are many Oracles among the Greeks, many also among the Egyptians, many in Africa, and many here in Asia. But these give responses neither without priests, nor without interpreters. Here, however, Apollo is self-moved, and performs the prophetic office wholly by himself; and this he does as follows. When he wishes to "communicate," he *moves in his place*, whereupon the priests forthwith take him up. Or if they neglect to take him up, he sweats, and *comes forth into the middle of the room*, (ες μεσον ετι κινειται) when, however, others bear him upon their shoulders, he guides them, moving from place to place. At length the chief priest supplicating him, asks him all sorts of questions. If he does not assent he moves backwards; if he approves he impels forward those who bear him, like a charioteer. Thus they arrive at responses. They do nothing except by this method. Thus he gives *predictions concerning the seasons, foretells storms, &c.* I will relate another thing also, which he did *in my presence*. The priests were bearing him upon their shoulders—he left them below upon the ground, while he himself *was borne aloft and alone into the air*," (Lucian. de Syria Dea)

Here now is a hint which ought not to be lost. A method suggested in which the prescient spirits may make themselves useful to mankind, and at the same time enrich their friends, —a kind of benevolence which we are told they like to indulge in. Let them make a *reliable* almanac, or almanacs, calculated for various meridians, and with tables of the weather for each day, or each week; surely, the books, if found to predict truly, would become right saleable,—a good speculation for some of the publishers for the spirits,—but, if they cannot inform us correctly in regard to the future of this world, let us be cautious how we trust them in regard to the next.

Here we have also as good a specimen of what "a piece of wood" can do, if it were wood, as any modern table or other furniture has exhibited hitherto, not excepting the table that went out at the window, or the bell that the Judge saw float over the heads of the company, ringing itself as it went.— The old spirits could also play on musical instruments as well as the new ones.

"The brazen statue of Memnon *which held a harp*, at certain hours emitted musical sounds. (canebat) Cambyses commanded it to be opened, suspecting some hidden mechanism within. Nevertheless, the statue, which had been consecrated with magic rites, after it had been opened, continued its music at the accustomed times." (Scholiastes Juvenalis.)

Some of the ancient statues could even speak, after a fashion.

" Concerning this statue, (of Apollo) where it stood, and how it spoke, I have said nothing. It is to be understood, however, that there was a statue at Delphi which emitted an *inarticulate* voice. For you must know that spirits speak with inarticulate voices because they have no organs by which they can speak articulately." (Nonnus)

This author seems not to have been well informed in regard

to the speaking powers of the spirits, since all ancient history declares that their voice was often heard in the air, speaking articulately, and repeating the same words in different places; and this was called, and universally known, by the name of "Vox Divina." In the case of the statue above mentioned, the spirit was evidently experimenting with the perverse material of which it was made, to see if he could make it articulate, as spirits now train the muscles which they wish to use for writing or speaking; but as the statue had no larynx or other organs of voice, as modern mediums have, the spirit found the solid stone (for the statue was probably of stone,) too inflexible for his purpose.

But not only the inanimate, wood and stone media—if it is proper to call those objects inanimate into which the spirits had been invoked and inchanted,—exhibited remarkable phenomena; the human, flesh-and-blood Mediums also, when the spirits had entered into them, gave wonderful physical manifestations of their presence.

"The signs, of those that are inspired, are multiform. For the inspiration is indicated by the motions of the (whole) body, and of certain parts of it, by the perfect rest of the body, by harmonious orders and dances, and by elegant sounds, (musical?) or the contraries of these. Either the body, likewise, is seen to be elevated, or increased in bulk, *or to be be borne along sublimely in the air.* An equability also of voice according to magnitude; or a great variety of voice after intervals of silence, may be observed. And again, sometimes the sounds have a musical intension and remission." (Iamblichus de Mysteriis.)

It seems it was not unusual for the Medium to become not merely clairvoyant, but meteoric also, so as quite to counterbalance and defy the law of gravity, just as happens to Mr.—— and some other modern Mediums. The "increase in bulk" also, is curious from its analogy to the blown-up condition of the Mediums in the middle ages, and indeed in more recent times, whereby they were unable to sink in water;—

which fact was observed also in very ancient times, as appears from the following quotation.

"These same people, moreover, (he is speaking of those who had the power of fascinating by the eye,) cannot be made to sink in water, even where weighed down by their (wet) clothes." (Phylarchus apud Plin. Nat. Hist. vii. 2.)

As we must suppose the spirits to operate by, and according to, the laws of nature, it seems likely that they produce these meteoric effects by retaining, or generating, within the bodies of those manifesting such marvellous specific levity, the requisite quantity of hydrogen, comparatively little when they are only to swim, but a good deal, one would think, and pretty well compressed, when they are to become lighter than atmospheric air. It is also apparent from the "great variety of voice," spoken of by Iamblichus, that several spirits could possess the medium at the same time, or in succession at the same sitting, or at least, such is the present explanation of similar changes of voice. The manifestations related by Iamblichus will do very well for Egypt, which had anciently great reputation in that line. India however, seems to have been the birthplace and cradle of the science of spirit-intercourse, and spirit-influence and phenomena. Egypt was but an imperfect and far-off imitator, as appears from the dispute of Apollonius Tyanensis with the Egyptian gymnosophists. (Philostrat. Apollon. Tyan. Vita Lib. vi. c. 11) The sages of India were, apparently, at all times, clairvoyant, and meteoric, or possessed of the power of rising into the air, whenever they chose to exercise it. The following, from an eye witness, beats Egypt entirely, and quite distances the doings of all the modern spirits of whom I have any definite knowledge.

"I have seen, said Apollonius, the Brahmins of India, dwelling on the earth and not on the earth, living fortified without fortifications, possessing nothing, and yet everything. This he spoke somewhat ænigmatically; but Damis (the companion of his journey to India) says they sleep upon the ground, but that the earth furnishes them with a grassy couch of whatever plants they desire, That he himself had seen them, *elevated two cubits above the surface of the earth, walk in the air!* not for the purpose of display, which was quite foreign to the character of the men; but because whatever they did, elevated, in common with the Sun, above the earth, would be more acceptable to that Deity. * * * * * * * Having bathed, they formed a choral circle, having Iarchas for their coryphæus, and striking the earth with their divining rods, *it rose up,* no otherwise than does the sea under the power of the wind, *and caused them to ascend into the air.* Meanwhile they continued to chant a hymn not unlike the paean of Sophocles which is sung at Athens in honor of Aesculapius. When they had descended &c." (Philostrat. Vita Apollon. Tyanens. Lib. iii. c. 15, 17.)

Thus much may suffice for this kind of physical manifestations, although I have passed by many recorded and well attested facts still more extraordinary; but I do not choose to bring forward anything which might prove incredible in the present stage of our own development. It were a pleasant and edifying sight, to behold a modern Circle floating in the air, and gyrating around their Medium, while they chant a hymn of invocation to their Spirit-President. When we have attained to this point of imitation, antiquity will set us still more difficult lessons.

The next class of physical manifestations of which I shall give some specimens, is that of the luminous appearances now called galvanic, magnetic, or odic lights, which sometimes assume shadowy spectral forms. These seem to have attended the ancient spirit-intercourse more commonly, and more remarkably, than they have hitherto done in the present iteration of it.

We have seen that the prophetess at Branchidæ became *encircled with light* during her preparations to give responses;—the same thing happened to the Pythia according to Iamblichus. "The prophetess at Delphi, whether, by means of the thin and fiery vapor which proceeds from the mouth of the cavern, she gives oracles to men ; or whether, from the Adytum, sitting upon a brazen tripod, or upon a four-footed stool sacred to the god, she delivers responses ; in either case, she gives herself up wholly to the divine influence, *and becomes effulgent with rays of light.*" (απο τε του πυρος άκτινος καταυγαζεται) (Iamblichus de Mysteriis) This manifestation of luminous appearances must have been quite common anciently, if indeed, not an *invariable* attendant upon the presence of true and good spirits ; though not always visible except to the Mediums, as perhaps is implied in the following extract :—

" But a species of fire is seen by the recipient, prior to the spirit being received, which sometimes becomes manifest to all the spectators, either when the numen is descending or when he is departing. * * * Those, however, who without these blessed spectacles, draw down spirits *invisibly*, are without vision, as if they were in the dark, and know nothing of what they do, except some small signs which become visible through the body of him who is divinely inspired, (the Medium) and certain other things which are manifestly seen, but they are ignorant of all the most important particulars of divine inspiration, which are concealed from them in the invisible." (Iambl. de Myst.) These lights, which were sometimes a mere halo, and sometimes spectral appearances, or apparitions, were a manifestation of the utmost practical importance, inasmuch as, by them, was to be determined the character of the spirit in possession of the Medium. I would commend this method to the early and careful consideration of the present Circles, since they seem to have great difficulty on this point, and are often led into uery amusing, not only, but vexatious, and expensive, mistakes, (See Supernal Theology) for want of some such scientific test of the character of the spirits. In order, therefore, to relieve the circles of such annoying inconveniences in future, and to hasten their development in this direction, I will furnish them, from the highest authority, with the scientific test they are so much in need of, while, at the same time I accomplish my purpose of giving a view of this class of phenomena in the ancient period.

"What is the indication of a god, or angel, or archangel, or demon, or a certain archon, or a soul being present? For to speak boastingly, and to exhibit a *phantasm* of a certain quality, is *common to gods and demons*, and to all the more excellent genera." (Porphyry to the Egyptian Anebo.)

The subject must have excited the same questions, and questioning, formerly as at present; however, Iamblichus throws great *light* upon it in his answer to the above query, as follows:—

"The phantasms, or luminous appearances, of the gods are uniform, those of demons are various; * * * those of souls are all-various. And the phasmata, indeed, of the gods will be seen shining with a salutary light; those of archangels will be terrible; those of angels more mild; those of demons will be dreadful; those of heroes are milder than those of demons; those of archons produce astonishment; and those of souls are similar to the heroic phasmata. The phasmata of the gods are entirely immutable according to magnitude, form, and figure; those of archangels fall short in sameness; * * * * those of demons are, at different times seen in a different form, and appear at one time great, and at another time small, yet are still recognized to be the phasmata of demons; * * * * * and those of souls imitate in no small degree the demoniacal mutations. * * * * * In the forms of the gods which are seen by the eyes the most clear spectacles of truth are perceived; * * * the images of demons are obscure; * * * * * and the images of souls appear to be *of a shadowy form*.

Again the *fire* of the gods appears to be entirely stable; that of archangels is tranquil; but that of angels is stably moved. The fire of demons is unstable; but that of heroes is, for the most part, rapidly moved. The fire of those archons that are of the first rank is tranquil; but of those that are of the last order is tumultuous; and the fire of souls is transmuted in a multitude of motions."

The *light* also, from the different orders of spirits produces different physical effects upon the beholders. The moral effect of the vision of the different orders is also different. All these different appearances, and their effects, are to be accurately observed, by those who would not fall into fatal errors and delusions: "For (hear, hear, and mark,) when a certain error happens in the theurgic art, and not such autoptic, or self-visible, images are seen as ought to occur, but others instead of these, then, *inferior powers* assume the form of the more venerable orders, *and pretend to be those whose forms they assume*, and hence, arrogant words are uttered by them, and such as exceed the authority they possess. * * * much falsehood is derived from the perversion which it is necessary the priests *should learn from the whole order of the phasmata*, by the proper observation of which, they are able to *confute and reject* the fictitious pretexts of those inferior powers, as by no means pertaining to true and good spirits." (Iamblichus de Mysteriis.)

"That, however, which is the greatest thing, is this, that he who draws down a certain divinity, sees a spirit descending and entering into some one, recognizes its magnitude and quality; and from this spectacle the greatest truth and power of the god, and especially the order he possesses, as likewise about what particulars he is adapted to speak the truth, what the power is which he imparts, and what he is able to effect, *become known to the scientific*." (Idem Ibidem.)

These rules imply that such lights, phantasms, "livid flames," or spectral appearances, were the usual, and that they ought to be, the *constant* attendants upon spirit-intercourse. They are also sufficiently definite and precise, *undoubtedly*, to serve instead of spirit-credentials, in the hands of the "scientific." But let the inexperienced, and those who have more curiosity than caution, beware of spirits who refuse to show their *light;*—they are, of course, spirits of *darkness.* That these rules are capable of answering the purpose for which they were intended, of determining the character and quality of a "self-visible spirit," is proved and illustrated by the following example of their application :—

"A certain Egyptian priest, who at that time was at Rome, and who became known to Plotinus through one of his friends, being desirous to exhibit his wisdom in that illustrious city, persuaded our philosopher to attend him, for the purpose of beholding, through his invocations, his familiar demon; to which request Plotinus readily consented. But the invocation was performed in the temple of Isis; this being the only pure place in Rome the Egyptian priest was able to find. However, instead of a demon, as was expected, a god approached, who was not in the genus of demons. The Egyptian, astonished at the unexpected event, exclaimed, "Happy Plotinus! who hast a god for a demon, and whose familiar attendant does not rank among the inferior kind." (Porphyr. Vita Plotin.) The practiced eye of the priest at once detected the rank and quality of the spirit, doubtless by the character of the light by which he made himself visible.

Here, now, is something which begins to look like science. Something by which the *"real* reality" and actual character of the spirits and of their communications may be tried and tested. Here is a veritable *science* of spiritism, reliable and appropriate. But, without "the glimmering of these livid flames," all is darkness; and without accurate distinction, and scientific appreciation of their different shades, motions, and effects upon the beholders, both physical and psychical, all is still uncertainty. Such being the result, anciently, and the successful and satisfactory result—for Iamblichus says the true theurgist would laugh at the attempt of evil dæmons to deceive him—of five hundred years of investigation and scientific experiment ; what rashness in our modern beginners, mere sophomores in this abstrusest of all the sciences, viz: η επιςημη των ψευδων και ψευδοντων !---what rashness ! to go on stumbling—as many, nay most, do go on—without the guidance of those various and peculiar subternal phosphorescences which are the natural lights and safety-lamps of the region under exploration.

CHAPTER VIII.

> For rather er he shulde faile,
> With *nicromance* he wolde assaile,
> To make his incantation.
>
> GOWER.

> Lamps must be solemnly burned before it; and then, after some diabolical exorcisms *necromantically* performed, the head shall prove vocal.
>
> GREGORY, POSTHUM.

In the examples of divination and other manifestations which have been related, little has been said in regard to the character or rank of the spirits whose presence was supposed to be necessary to the phenomena. Ancient opinions varied on this point. By some it was held that they were all spirits of dead men (Euhemerus et alii) not even excepting the gods themselves, who, by a gradual process going on for ages, like unto certain geological changes, came at length to be fully transformed, from simple ghosts, unto the nature of deity. Indeed the process was going on pretty rapidly before their eyes, as in such cases as those of Hercules and Aesculapius, and others, not to mention those mushroom gods, the dead Roman Emperors, who sprang up in a night, from beasts, into divinities, demanding their temples and altars, and giving oracles in competition with Apollo himself.

The prevailing belief, however, was that there were several orders of gods, then heroes, demons, and *souls*. Which last were not necessarily spirits of the dead, because all ancient souls were pre-existent like Dr. Beecher's, and Spirit-Swedenborg's (Celestial Telegraph,) and a soul communicating thro' a medium, or a simulacrum, might be one which had not yet "descended into matter," or it might be the spirit of a dead man; probably the rules, of which Iamblichus has given us a specimen, enabled "the scientific" to distinguish the one kind from the other. But however much the gods or unembodied souls may have been consulted; the disembodied souls, or spirits of the dead, seem to have been, anciently, as now, the favorite source of information, especially in the private Circles and Sittings. Perhaps there was some feeling of restraint and hesitation in regard to calling familiarly, in a private way and not in their public temples, upon the "Great Gods," as, in our time, I believe, the Almighty, and even the Angels, are not commonly sent for to answer questions.

The common belief of the ancients in regard to the relation of the living to their dead ancestors was also extremely favorable to the prevalence of this kind of spirit-intercourse. The subjoined extract gives a very good idea of that belief especially among the Romans. We see here that the term demon may mean also a spirit of the dead.

"There is also a second class of dæmons viz: the souls of those who having lived meritoriously have departed from the body. Such a soul I find called in the ancient Latin tongue *Lemur*. Of these Lemures, he, who having obtained by lot the guardianship of his posterity, presides over the house with a quiet and placable superintendence is called the household Lar. But those, who, on account of a vicious life, having obtained no happy seats, are a sort of vagabonds, or are punished by a kind of exile; and who inflict idle terrors upon good men, but more real evils upon the wicked;—this kind is commonly called Larvæ. But inasmuch as it is uncertain which of these kinds has fallen to the lot of any one, whether it may be a Lar or a Larva, he is called the god Manes, Manem Deum,—the appellation god being added by way of respect. Because, of those belonging to this class, those only are considered gods who having passed through life with wisdom and justice, and being afterwards supposed by men to possess divine powers, are honored with fanes and religious ceremonies; as Amphiaraus in Boeotia; in Africa Mopsus; in Egypt Osiris; others in other places, and Aesculapius everywhere. But this whole order of dæmons consists of those who were once in human bodies." (Apuleius de Deo Socratis.)

These last, the spirits of distinguished men, had everywhere their public fanes and temples, or more humble places of resort, where they could be at all times consulted,—as Swedenborg and Dr. Franklin, and especially our defunct M. D's will have in due time; we already have panpsychia, or places consecrated to spirits in general, and each will be sure to claim his separate, and appropriate, honors shortly,—the whole world was crowded with them, "stipatus est orbis," says an ancient writer. But above all others Aesculapius was everywhere in demand and repute. This man had been a physician in his life-time of considerable business and reputation; but his post-mortem practice was one of incredible extent,—the poor spirit must have had a weary travel of it even for a spirit, to attend at all his offices as often as he was called for,—with an ever increasing fame, justly due,—as appeared from innumerable tablets suspended in his temples by grateful patients, describing their disease, giving the prescription, and recording the cure,—to remarkable success. A fact, this success, not at all incredible, or likely to be doubted, by any one competent to form a correct opinion. This is plain from the record of his cases. Most of these invaluable documents have perished through time and the envy of the Christians.— A few however remain, of which the following are a specimen:—

" At this very time the Oracle gave response to Caius who was blind: 'That he should approach the sacred altar; that he should kneel; that from the right side he should come to the left, and place five fingers upon the altar, and raise his hand, and place it upon his eyes.' And his sight was fully restored, the people being present and congratulating."

" To Lucius afflicted with pain in the side and despaired of by all men, the god gave response: 'That he should approach the altar, and take ashes, and mix with wine and place upon his side.' And he recovered, and publicly returned thanks to the god, and the people congratulated him."

" To Julianus vomiting blood and despaired of by all men, the god gave response from the oracle; 'that he should approach the altar and take the cones of the pine (or seeds of the pine cone, κοκκους ϲροβιλου) and eat them three days with honey.' And he recovered and publicly returned thanks to the god."

"To Valerius Aper, a blind soldier, the oracle gave response; 'that he should take the blood of a white cock and honey, and rub them together, and therewith anoint his eyes three days.' And he saw, and came, and gave thanks &c."— (Gruteri Thesaurus.)

No other disembodied response-giving spirit was, perhaps, quite as ubiquitous as that of Aesculapius, but their number and distribution were such as to be quite sufficient for the accommodation of the public, without the trouble of much travel, either on the part of the spirits or of the public. From the ancient Orpheus ,whose skull gave responses in a cave at Lesbos, (Philostratus in Heroicis) down to the last dead Emperor, or emperor's mistress, the host of publicly vaticinating spirits of the dead, had become prodigiously great.

But, besides all these, there were more private methods of "*holding conversation with the shades* and spirits of the deceased," (Plinius Nat. Hist. Lib. xxx. v.) methods which were reckoned magical, as we have seen in the case of the enchanted boys. By this method spirits could be evoked at pleasure, and sent on errands as is the present fashion. "Apion said that he could call up spirits and send them to ask Homer of what country he was, and who were his parents, but that he did not dare to divulge the answer." (Idem xxx. vi.)

These magic arts of divination including necromancy, or divination by the dead, were taught among the arcana of the temples, and constituted a part of the esoteric lessons of the philosophers who had traveled into Egypt and India to learn them. (Idem xxx. ii.) In the more ancient times these were strictly mystic and esoteric acquirements, but at a later period, Rome and the empire were filled with traveling magicians, and Egyptians, like unto our own traveling Mediums, who could fascinate, enchant, get responses from spirits, make visible one's attendant demon, and if their employer could furnish means for the requisite rites, would undertake to make the gods themselves obedient to his will.

This they attempted to do for Nero, who, unsatisfied to hold divided empire with Jupiter, was resolved to be sole monarch and to reign over gods also as well as men. (Plin. Nat. Hist. xxx. v.) However, the gods, with the aid of Galba, were more than a match for him and his magicians.

Now in order that we may not be overrun in like manner; that *every thing* may not be polluted with the slime of these "frogs of Egypt;" that we may avoid the abuses which anciently compelled the State so often to interfere; I would respectfully suggest to the fathers of the Republic, or, to whomsoever it may properly concern, that it may be well to have erected, and consecrated to particular spirits, a reasonable number of public fanes and temples, at convenient localities, and that these places have a monopoly of the spirit-business. For Apollo, we cannot do better, I think, than to take Swedenborg; and an excellent Pythia, to begin with, would be the lady who enacted Tom Jones, and the unhappy parson in Section Thirty-nine, (See Spiritualism.) For Aesculapius, let us, by all means, have Hahneman; because he could not only write prescriptions, but bring his medicines along with him; for the politicians, let them if possible, induce Marc Antony to come down; for the———— but details would be injudicious, perhaps dangerous. A Panpsychion here and there, where people could take their choice, might complete the establishment.

These ancient magicians or necromancers were not themselves Mediums, but rather what are now callled Mesmerizers or Magnetizers, operators who induced the magnetic and clairvoyant state, or caused the spirit to speak through the enchanted Medium, or to make himself visible, and show his colors, and the flag he sailed under. On great occasions, and where more mighty powers were to be evoked, the rites were not only very formal and mystic, but what were called "impious and horrid." The sacrifices must be of coal black animals, and sometimes even human victims were offered, as in the case of the Emperors Nero and Didius (Plin. Nat. Hist. & Spartian. Vit. Did. Jul.)

There were also mysterious words, or names, of which they made use, the bare utterance of which was sufficient to fix the sun in the heavens. The meaning of these names was altogether unknown to those who used them. They were not *without* meaning however, for listen to Iamblichus: "you inquire, he says, (in answer to Porphyry) *what efficacy there is in names that are not significant.* They are not however, without signification; but let them be indeed unknown to us, yet to the gods all of them are significant, though not according to an effable mode." (de Mysteriis) He proceeds to say however, that "some of them are known to us, the explications of which we receive from the gods." Perhaps some of the modern shades also can interpret them, if any one is curious on that point; perhaps also the Judge would like, *or would do well*, to make use of them, instead of the name of God, for the purpose of controling "unprogressed" and impudent spirits. The spirits will probably understand them as well as the gods did. The following is a list of some of the most potent of them, at the service of the Judge, or any other gentleman, whom vulgar spirits may treat disrespectfully : Meu, Threu, Mor, Phor, Teux, Za, Chri, Ge, Ze, Azulph, Znōn, Threux, Bain, Chōōk. (Alex. Trallian. Lib. ii.) Our apocatastatic spirit-period is but just commencing, and we have, evidently, much to learn yet. The use, and powers, of amulets and talismans are only just beginning to be reacknowledged, (Spirit Telegraph) but let the Circles develop the mysteries of these monosyllables, and wear them upon their seals, frontlets and phylacteries, if they would know their power over spirits, and the laws of nature, and understand the effects of a true talisman in ancient times. Some such vocable probably was the motto in the ring of Gyges ; nay, some one of these very names, perhaps Threux, or Chōōk, may have been the identical legend on the "Signet of Solomon."

In the ancient period however, just as in our own, a polite and well-developed Medium could hold conversation with the spirits of the departed at his pleasure, without any *spell* or apparatus of incantations, or other rites, holy or profane, except just to request the pleasure of their company. The following is a good specimen of this kind of dialogue, superior somewhat, as the reader will notice, in the character of the information imparted by the spirit, to its modern imitations. Scene, the tomb of Achilles on the plain of Troy.

"I," said he, (loquitur Apollonius Tyanensis) "did not, like Ulysses, dig a trench, and evoke the shades with the blood of lambs, in order to be admitted to conversation with Achilles ; but making use of a prayer such as the Sages of India think proper for the invocation of heroes, *O, Achilles,* said I, *the many assert that you are dead, but I do not coincide with that opinion, neither does Pythagoras my Master. If we are right show us your shadow.* (δειξον ἡμιν το σεαυτου ειδος) *For allow me to say that my eyes might be of much service to you, could you use them as witnesses of your being alive.*

Thereupon there was a slight quaking of the mound, and it gave forth the form of a young man of five cubits in height, dressed in a Thessalian cloak, but not exhibiting the haughtiness of demeanor which some ascribe to Achilles. The countenance was severe (δεινος) yet not in a way to diminish its beauty, which seems to me never to have been duly described, though Homer said much concerning it. It was of that indescribable character that every attempt to pourtray it must necessarily come short of the reality. Appearing at first, as I mentioned, of five cubits, he immediately enlarged himself to more than twice that size, so that when fully expanded he was twelve cubits in height, and his beauty had increased in the same proportion. His hair spoke for itself that it had never been cut, * * * and the first beard of youth was upon his chin. "I am happy to meet you," said he, "for I have, this long time, needed such a man as you are. The Thessalians have, these many years neglected the sepulcral rites due to me. Nevertheless I have been unwilling to take offence. For if I should once become angry it would be worse for them than for the Greeks who formerly perished in this place. Remind them in a friendly way of their neglect, and that they ought not to show themselves worse than these Trojans, who notwithstanding I killed so many of them, offer to me public sacrifices and fruits of the season, and supplicate from me reconciliation and forgiveness, which I will never grant them. For their perjuries against me will not permit that Ilium should be ever restored to its ancient condition, or flourish again as many subverted cities have done, but it shall forever remain as if it were but yesterday destroyed. Lest now I subject the Thessalians to the same punishment, be my ambassador to them in regard to the matter I spoke of." I will be your ambassador, said I, for the scope of the message is that they should take care of themselves. But I desire, O Achilles, a favor of you. "Ah! I understand," said he, "you wish to ask about Trojan matters, ask therefore five questions, whatever you please and the fates permit."

And first, I inquired if he were buried in the way described by the poets. "I am buried," said he, "in a way very agreeable to me and to Patroclus, we were very intimate in our youth, and now the same golden urn contains us both as if we were one. As to the lament which they say the Muses and Nereids made for me;—the Muses have never been at this place, but the Nereids do still occasionally come here." I then inquired if Polyxena were sacrificed to him. He said that story was true, that she was not, however, put to death by the Greeks, but that, of her own choice, in honor of their mutual love, she fell upon a sword at his tomb. For the third question I inquired; did Helen, O, Achilles, ever go to Troy? or was that a fiction of Homer? "For a long time," said he, "we were deceived, sending ambassadors to the Trojans, and fighting them on her account, while we supposed she was there. She, in the mean time, was in Egypt, whither, she was abducted by Paris. When we became aware of this we fought the remainder of the time for Troy itself, that we might not go home in disgrace." I had arrived at the fourth question, and said, I was astonished that Greece could have produced so many, and such men, as Homer marshals against Troy. "The barbarians," replied he, "were not much our inferiors, so prolific was the whole earth, at that time, of the manly virtues." (Manifestly one of Plato's fertile periods, as Mr. Thomas Taylor also thinks, which terminated when our own apocatastatic predecessor commenced, at the "mournful sound of the trumpet" in Sylla's time.) For the fifth question I said, how happened it that Homer was ignorant of Palamedes? or if he were not ignorant, why did he not speak of him in the poem of which you were the subject. "If Palamedes had not come to Troy," answered Achilles, "Troy never would have been burnt. Since, however, a man eminent in counsel, and a capital warrior, was slain in order to please Ulysses, Homer did not introduce him into the poem that he might not be compelled to blame Ulysses." And Achilles lamented him as among the greatest and fairest, conspicuous in youth and warlike virtues, in temperance superior to all others, and intimate with the Muses. "Thou, therefore, O, Apollonius,—for the wise are dependant in some sort upon the wise—look after his tomb, and restore the statue of Palamedes which is shamefully fallen down. It lies in Aulis, over against Methymna." So saying, with a middling smart flash of lightning, (αςραπη μετρια) he departed." (Philostrat. Vita Apollon. Tyanens. L. iv. c. 16.)

Perhaps, considering my promise to be brief, facts and phenomena sufficient for my purpose have now been detailed; and I think it has been made plain that they were, in ancient times, and in the heathen world, essentially the same in kind, that they took place under essentially the same circumstances, and that they were owing to essentially the same causes, as in the spirit-epidemic of the present time. Let us make out a catalogue of the ancient manifestations, and see whether it will not answer as well for the modern phenomena. Under the head of physical manifestations we find:

Lights, both fixed, and moved.
Halo, encircling the Medium.
Spectra, luminous, or otherwise visible; self-visible Spirits.
Sounds, cries, voices in the air, trumpets, speaking spectres, musical intonations, musical instruments played.
Inert bodies moved, and suspended in the air.
Mediums suspended, and moving in the air.

The physiological manifestations were:

Trance,—Magnetic sleep,—Magnetic insensibility.

The psychological, or physiologico-psychological, were:

Spirit-speaking,—Spirit-writing.
Speaking unknown languages.
Answering mental questions.
Clairvoyance, both in relation to time, and space.
Magnetization, by the eye, the hand, by music, and by water.
Spirits answering questions through Mediums, and without Mediums.

The ancient heathen life, and heathen mind, especially about the time of the commencement of Christianity, were, so to speak, saturated with these things. They constituted a part of their daily faith and practice. They were also not unknown, though they had always been discountenanced, and forbidden, among the Jews. And notwithstanding Christ and the Apostles rebuked and repressed them in every form, and inculcated principles which tended to eradicate them from the heart and life of Christians; yet, soon after the Apostles' time, many found their way into the Church who did not leave behind them their heathen belief, or practice, in regard to these things. Hence the Church suffered and was annoyed, mainly from the fact, that some of the injudicious and unapostolic successors of the apostles attempted to make use of some of these manifestations for the interest of the Church. Finding it easier to let down the Church half way to paganism, than to bring paganism up, from its wholly sensuous forms of life, even in its religion, to walk by faith in that which was invisible, and otherwise wholly supersensuous. The Church, therefore, had its prophetesses and other clairvoyant young ladies, a sort of christian Pythonesses, until, by sad experience, it learned to drive them back to the heathendom which was their proper home. Alas! from that time to the present, the Church has suffered more than from all other causes together, from that most easy of all errors to fall into, and the most difficult to be extricated, or to extricate ones self, from;—the error of *mistaking the merely physiological for the truly spiritual.* But I am anticipating what I intend to say, bye and bye, in a seperate chapter.

CHAPTER IX.

Is there any one, O Melitus, who acknowledging that there are humane *things, can yet deny that there are any* men *? or, confessing that there are* equine *things, can nevertheless deny that there are any* horses *? If this cannot be, then no man who acknowledges* demonial *things, can deny* demons.

CUDWORTH, INTELLECTUAL SYSTEM, p. 254.

Now if there be no *spirit*, matter must of necessity move itself.

H. MORE, IMMORTALITY OF THE SOUL.

What was, in the ancient period, the explanation given of the phenomena we have been considering? how were they accounted for? In ancient times, just as now, there were three opinions on this point. There were those, among both heathens and christians, who asserted that all was the effect of mere craft and fraud. Then there were the physicists, or physiologists, who accounted for the facts by supposing certain arcane laws of Nature and of the nervous system. Then the spiritists, who were as positive and dogmatical at that time, as they are at present. And then there was a fourth class, as now, who declined to have any decided opinion. Of those holding these various mental relations to the phenomena the believers in the spirits were by far the most numerous. These included the great masses of the people in all countries. Indeed, to doubt, in regard to many of these manifestations, was to be an infidel, in the most opprobrious sense, and to deny the religion of one's country. Hence the popular hatred against the Epicureans, who, as a sect, held that the gods, if there were gods, like Gallio, " cared for none of these things ;" and as for the spirits of dead men, there were none, and therefore they were not likely to act or to speak with or without Mediums. These opinions excited so much odium that the Epicureans were often driven from the temples ; for the ancient spirits and their friends had the same antipathy towards the incredulous as their modern successors. Yet some, even of these, probably believed in the existence and *influence of evil spirits;* with their great progenitor Democritus, who seems to have been himself a sort of Medium, or experimenter upon others, in a private way. (Plutarch, ut supra, & Plin. Nat. Hist. Lib. xxx.) Let us look at some of the language of the unbelievers. Hear Cicero, who however, was not an Epicurean.

" Neither do I reckon that any faith ought to be had in the prophets of Mars, or in the revelations of Apollo, (the responses of the Pythia,) some of which are the merest fiction, some, *inconsiderate babble*, (how perfectly apocatastatic !) never of any authority with a man of even moderate capacity. * * * O, sacred Apollo, Chrysippus filled a whole volume with your oracles, partly false, in my opinion, and partly, by accident, true,—as happens in all treatises, for the most part, —partly equivocal and obscure, so that the Interpreter needs to be interpreted, and the lot itself needs to be referred to the lot.', (De Divinatione, lib. ii.)

In another part of the same treatise, speaking of those who accounted for the inferiority of the Delphic Oracle in his time to its former fame, by supposing that the vapor from the cavern had become diminished in quantity, or deteriorated in quality, (probably its varying reputation was owing to the fact that sometimes the Pythia happened to be a " well developed," and at others an "imperfectly-developed," Medium,) he says : " I know not how it is that these superstitious, and all but fanatical philosophers, seem to desire nothing so much as that they may be made fools of. They will rather suppose that to have become extinct, which if it had ever been, must have been always, than not believe that which is altogether incredible." (Idem Ibidem.)

Some of the early Christians also were incredulous in regard to the agency of spirits in causing the phenomena, although most of them retained their former spiritism, but after their conversion, believed that the spirits concerned in these manifestations, were *all evil* spirits. The christian unbelievers were sometimes severe upon such men as our friend Iamblichus, and other operators.

" Away with your Egyptian mysteries, and Etruscan *necromancy*. (conversing with the spirits of the dead,) These, undoubtedly, are the impious arts, of infidel men (pagans) for the purposes of deception, invented for pure unmingled fraud." (Clemens Alexandrinus, Stromat. Lib. iii.)

" I could adduce many things from Aristotle and the Peripatetics subversive of faith in the Pythia and the other oracles; and show that the Greeks themselves had no confidence in them, even in the most famous of them. But if we admit that they were not the mere craft and tricks of men ; if we concede that they were really oracles, it does not necessarily follow that any divinity presided over them, but rather, certain wicked Dæmons, and spirits hostile to the human race." (Origen contra Celsum, Lib. vii.)

Those who believed, or suspected, that the facts were explainable without the agency of spirits, and who admitted that they were more than mere fraud, did not, however, attempt to point out very definitely *how*, or by what laws of nature, they were to be explained. So, I believe, those of parallel opinion at present, throw a very obscure and uncertain light upon the subject, when they attempt to give us the law of it; just enough to make the darkness visible. They speak of abnormal states of the nervous system, and contagious sympathies, and electricity, and galvanism, magnetism, and *od*, in a very odd way; for while they assure us that these are sufficient to account for the facts, they do not indicate to us *how*, by them, any of the facts are to be accounted for. The ancients, I think, conjectured more philosophically than we; except where we, not merely apocatastatically, but very plagiaristically, bring forward the identical dogmas of the ancients as our own.

" Concerning the causes of divination, it is dubious whether a god, an angel, or a demon, or some other power, is present in manifestations. Or does the soul assert and imagine these things, *or are they, as some think, the passion of the soul, excited from small incentives?* Or is a certain mixed form of subsistence produced from our soul and divine inspiration externally derived." (Porphyry to the Egyptian Anebo.)

Another, who seems to have investigated the subject pretty carefully, after acknowledging that the " manifestations" are under the general superintendence of certain " mediate powers" (medias potestates) offers at the same time, the following conjectural natural explanation of them.

" I am however, inclined to think, (quin et illud mecum reputo) that the human mind, and especially the ingenuous mind of the young, can, by the soothing or evoking power (evocamento) of song, or by the lulling influence of odors, be brought into a state analogous to that of sleep, (soporari) and be, as it were, driven into an oblivion of things present; and so, being, for a short time, removed from the remembrance of the body, it is restored, and returns, to its natural, that is, divine and immortal relations, and thereby becomes prescient of the future." (clairvoyant) (Apuleius de Magia Oratio.)— This is evoking the spirit out of the Medium instead of invoking a spirit into him; yet it *looks like* an explanation of the phenomena.

"The human mind draws, and is replenished from the divine, and since all things are full and saturated with a divine sense and intellect, it follows that the human mind from its relation of kindred (*cognatione*) with the divine, may be moved in sympathy, or unison therewith. (*commoveri*) Persons in the waking state, however, are busy about the necessities of life, and so no longer partake of the divine consciousness, impeded by corporeal restraints. But some few there are who can evoke themselves out of the body, and are rapt away into a knowledge of things divine." (Cicero de Divinatione, Lib. i.)

This is as good, as the all-pervading magnetic aura which is capable of becoming a medium of universal knowledge to all souls which can get out of the opake and impervious body, into it.

"Wherefore those, whose souls, contemning the body, fly forth, and make excursions without, doubtless, excited, and inflamed, by a certain ardor, *behold* the things which they communicate in the vaticinating state. And such minds which do not *inhere* in the body, are thus excited (to go forth) by many things; as in the case of those who are thus excited by a certain sound of voices, and by Phrygian chants." (Idem Ibidem.)

The following, however, is admirably adapted to the explanation of modern manifestations, since it does not seem to imply the necessity of going out of the body in order to come *en rapport* with the soul of the world as the medium of common or universal consciousness.

"This being posited and conceded that there is a certain divine energy which includes within itself the human life, it is not difficult to conjecture a way to account for such things (in relation to divination, augury &c) as we do actually see to take place. For even for choosing the proper animal for sacrifice, (for instance, so that the omens would correspond to the future event,) *the directing agency may be a certain sen-*

tieut power (vis quædam sentiens) *which pervades the whole universe.*" (Idem Ibidem.)

Here is a sort of perceptive fluid abundant enough for every body to partake of, and as convenient as *od*, or as the " pantheaprinciple ! !" a kind of universal sensorium, or sea of sense, though it does not appear how its undulations are to come in contact and mingle, with the thinking fluid of individuals, except in the case of the crack-brained. For the supposition that this sentient principle is so subtle as to pass through all sorts of craniums would prove too much,—we should all be clairvoyant.

These ancient explanatory theories, however, were brought forward with great modesty, and with much more of diffidence than dogmatism. Not so the Spiritists,—they spoke with undoubting confidence, sure that the evidence for the correctness of their view of the subject did not fall short of demonstration. With the confidence of truth ; probably their successors will say. But unluckily for that kind of confirmation of their opinion, the believers in the theory of fraud and collusion and self-deception were equally confident. Some of the believers however, as at present, spoke doubtingly enough.

" Whether these things were true, and in what degree, I dispute not; men, indeed, accounted them, and believed in them as true; insomuch that those skilful in divination were held in such esteem as even to be thought worthy to reign; —the men namely who make known to us the divine precepts and monitions, both while living and *after they are dead.*"— (Strabo, Geograph. Lib. xvi.)

It was the opinion of Pythagoras " that the regions of the air are filled with spirits, who are demons and heroes; that from them come all kinds of divination, omens &c; that all kinds of divination are to be held in honor." (Vita Pythag. apud Diogin. Laert.)

" There are collections of excellent arguments of the philosophers in favor of the reality of divination. Among whom, that I may speak of the most ancient, the Colophonian Xenophanes alone, of those who admitted the existence of the gods, wholly rejected divination. All the rest, with the exception of Epicurus *babbling about the nature of the gods*, approved it, but not by the same methods. For while Socrates and the Socratics, Zeno and his successors, the old Academy and the Peripatetics consenting, remained in the faith of the ancient philosophers; the well-known views of Pythagoras, and of Democritus, adding great weight to this opinion; Dicæarchus the Peripatetic rejected all other modes of divination, but retained that by dreams, and by *fury;*—furor, the "trance or interior state," which seems to have been very energetic anciently, hence called rage, and fury. This was the method of the Sibyls, who were said to speak "with insane mouth;" of the Pythia; of the enchanted; and of those who under the influence of the theurgic art "energize enthusiastically."

"As to what was said, however, in regard to the dæmons (δαιμονες) forsaking and deserting the Oracles, so that they lie idle, like the unused tools of the mechanic;—there is involved here a different and more important question, namely, by what powers and methods are these spirits enabled to excite in persons of both sexes, enthusiasm, prophetic rage, and a knowledge of the future. For we cannot attribute the silence of the Oracles to the departure of the spirits unless we understand how by their presence they rendered them vocal.

"Do you think then," rejoined Ammonius, "that the spirits are anything else than wandering Souls, "*air-clothed*," as Hesiod says? For my part, I am of opinion, that, just as a man acting tragedy or comedy differs from himself; so, a Soul wearing the dress of this body differs from itself. There is, therefore, nothing incredible in the supposition that (unembodied) Souls *in communication with* (embodied) souls can impart to them a knowledge of the future, as we make known to each other many things by looks gestures &c., without the use of the voice."

"But if," said I, "the souls which are disembodied, or which never have been embodied, are dæmons, and terrestrial guardians of mortal men, as you and Hesiod suppose; why do we deprive souls in the body of that faculty by which dæmons are naturally enabled to foreknow and make known future events? For it is not likely that souls on leaving the body acquire any new properties or endowments which they did not possess before, but that they always possessed them, though of inferior quality while mixed with the body. As the sun does not appear in its splendor when behind the clouds, but, though always the same, yet is for us obscured or invisible; so the soul does not then first acquire its power of divination when it emerges from the body as from a cloud, but this faculty is already in its possession, however darkened and rendered imperfect, by being commixed and mingled with a mortal nature." (Plutarch. De Oraculorum Defectu.)

This is a little pro, and a little con., precisely like a modern discussion of the same subject. It would seem likely, however, on the whole, that the embodied soul may, by certain excitations, or evocations, be enabled to resume pretty fully, its inherent and natural, though ordinarily latent power of prescience.

But the most positive witness on the other side, and properly so, as he testifies of his own experience and observation, is our *Expert*, Iamblichus. To give his evidence in full, would be to quote the whole treatise concerning the Mysteries of the Egyptians. A few extracts however, will be sufficient for my purpose. In answer to some doubting queries he says:

"The greatest remedy for all such doubts is this, to know *the principle of divination*, that it neither originates from bodies, nor from the passions about bodies, nor from a certain nature, and the powers about nature, nor from any human apparatus, or the habits pertaining to it. But neither does it originate from a certain art, externally acquired. For the whole authority of it pertains to the gods, (vernacule, spirits) and is imparted by them. * * * *nor in short, is it a human work, but is divine and supernatural, and is supernally sent to us from the heavens."* (De Mysteriis.)

This is quite satisfactory. It is always refreshing to find a man who has an opinion of his own,—so vanburenish is the majority of men on important subjects—such positive people, however, as in the present instance, are apt to deal more in assertions than reasons.

Here is a good specimen of an ancient Medium in a *theopemptic* trance, or in the "interior state."

"And sometimes, indeed, an invisible and incorporeal spirit surrounds the recumbents, so as not to be perceived by the sight, *but by a certein other co-sensation and intelligence.* (how exact our apocatastatic iterations!) The entrance of this spirit also is *accompanied with a noise,* (does he *rap* when he comes in, as our spirits do?) and he diffuses himself on all sides without any contact, and effects admirable works conducive to the liberation of the passions of the soul and body. But sometimes a bright and tranquil light shines forth, by which the sight of the eyes is detained, and which occasions them to become closed, though they were before open. The other senses however, are in a vigilant state, and in a certain respect have a co-sensation of the light unfolded by the gods, and the recumbents hear what the gods say."— (Clairvoyant, and clairaudient.) (Idem Ibidem.)

"If the presence of the fire of the gods, and a certain ineffable species of light (od) externally accede to him who is possessed, and if they wholly fill him, have dominion over, and circularly comprehend him on all sides, so that he is not able to exert any one energy of his own, what sense, or animadversion, or appropriate projection of intellect, can there be in him who receives a divine fire? What human motion, likewise, can then intervene, or what human reception of passion or extasy, or of aberration of the phantasy, or of anything else of the like kind can take place?" (why, plainly, *in that case,* none) (Idem Ibidem.)

"But it is necessary to investigate the causes of divine mania. And these are the illuminations proceeding from the gods, the spirits imparted by them, and the all-perfect domination of divinity, which comprehends, indeed, everything in us, but *exterminates entirely, our own proper consciousness and motion.* This divine possession, also, emits words which are not understood by those that utter them; for they pronounce them, as it is said, "with an insane mouth," and are wholly subservient, and entirely yield themselves to the energy of the predominating god." [Idem Ibidem.]

Hear also how readily he can silence objectors against what they are pleased to think undignified and unworthy manifestations, such as " divining from meal," moving about inanimate bodies, (scilicet, tables and such-like.)

" If, also, the power of the gods proceeds in pre-manifestation as far as to things inanimate, such as pebble stones, rods, *pieces of wood, &c.*, this very thing is most admirable, * * * because it *imparts soul to things inanimate, motion to things immoveable,* and makes all things to partake of reason, and to be defined by the measures of intellection, tho' possessing no portion of reason from themselves. * * * * For as the divinity sometimes makes some stupid man to speak wisely, (a Medium for instance) through which it becomes manifest to every one, that this not a certain human, but a divine work; thus, also, he reveals through things deprived of knowledge, (tables, for instance,) conceptions which precede all knowledge. And at the same time he declares to men that the signs which are exhibited are worthy of belief, and *that they are superior to nature.* Through them, also he inserts in us wisdom." (Idem Ibidem.)

Here now are reasons for, and an explanation of the causes of, the " physical manifestations," much more intelligible than any non-spiritist, ancient or modern, has given, or in my opinion, can give. And what matters it how trifling the phenomena, provided they are " superior to nature," and so manifest the power of the deity. Why should not a table speak foolishly ? the miracle consists in its *speaking*, and not in what it says. Anciently, however, as is plain from the above extract, " things deprived of knowledge" spake more wisely than at present, more wisely than they are likely to, at present, for we have the highest modern authority for saying that " it is an unwarrantable thing to look for instruction much superior to the mental development of the Medium." (The Present Age & Inner Life, p. 72.)

Now the mental development of a table, at least, of ordinary tables. must be somewhat in the incipient stage ; certain dining tables, card tables, and council tables, perhaps, may speak as well, or even better, than some of those who sit at them. But I am interrupting the witness. Speaking of some of the most distinguished of the public Mediums, of those who gave the oracular responses of the gods, our " Expert" is very definite and explicit.

" But this divine illumination is immediately present, and *uses the prophetess as an instrument* ; she neither being any longer mistress of herself, nor capable of attending to what she says, nor perceiving where she is. Hence after prediction she is scarcely able to recover herself." (Idem Ibidem.]

Here is a plenary inspiration not ashamed to assert itself; quite unlike our apologetic modern " not much superior to the mental development of the Medium," forsooth ! The fact of the character of modern inspiration is not, I think, to be denied ; it rests upon the very highest authority, that of a modern Expert ; but then, cui bono ? what is the use of such inspiration ? Anciently it was the spirit, and nothing but the spirit who spoke, the Medium furnished nothing except the vocal organs, hence some instruction worthy of the teacher was reasonably to be expected, for,

" She possesses the inspiration of the god shining into the pure seat of her soul, becomes full of an unrestrained afflatus, and receives the divine presence in a perfect manner, and without any impediment." [Idem Ibidem.]

So also the Pythia was a mere instrument, in the most literal and fullest sense.

"And when, indeed, fire ascending from the mouth of the cavern circularly invests her in collected abundance, she becomes filled from it with a divine splendour. But when she places herself upon the seat of the god, she becomes co-adapted to his stable prophetic power; and from both these preparatory operations she becomes wholly possessed by the god. And then, indeed, he is present with, and illuminates her in a separate manner; and is different from the fire, the vapor which ascends with it from the cavern, the proper seat, and in short, from all the visible apparatus of the place, whether physical or sacred." [Idem Ibidem.]

He is not only very positive in his direct assertions of the agency of spirits in the manifestations, but shows (to his own satisfaction) that all other theories are quite insufficient to account for them.

CHAPTER X.

POLL. Thou hast even now spoke, and that truly, that spacious is the Sea of various opinions concerning these Spirits; for so indeed it is; but what Port thou touchest at, I desire thee it may not seem troublesom to thee to tell me.

CAST. That which thou desirest, I conceive to be this; I hold that these tumultuous Spirits are mere images of Satan; which are not to be feared, neither is there any credit to be given to their answers.

A DISCOURSE OF THE NATURE OF SPIRITS.

Among those who agreed in referring the manifestations to the agency of spirits, there was anciently the same difference of opinion as at present, in regard to the *character* of the spirits; there was also the same agreement of opinion as now in regard to their character. They all agreed in believing that there were *evil spirits* concerned in the production of some of the phenomena; but they differed on the question whether they were *all* evil;—some asserting as now, that they were *all evil* spirits, and others holding, as at present, that they were part good and part evil. There has been, however, since that time, some "progress" in the mental development of this last class in regard to the *definition* of "evil." Anciently an evil spirit was very uncivilly called a *wicked* spirit, but now, such has been the "progress" of civilization, which "emollit animos nec sinit esse feros," that they are politely denominated unfortunate, undeveloped, "unprogressed," or sometimes, roguish, or mischievous, spirits. But anciently there was supposed to be,—except by the Epicureans " babbling about the nature of the gods"—a difference in kind between physical, or physiological, and moral relations —(I should have said spiritual relations, but *spiritual*, that word which used to stir one's deepest consciousness, has come to be an adjective which is used to qualify and define something relating to those most unspiritual of all disembodied, or unembodied agents who inspire very foolish people with that which is "not much superior to their own mental development." Let us therefore, as many as continue to believe in the being of anything truly spiritual, which is not merely a more diffuse and attenuated form of eternal and universal Matter, and in truly spiritual relations; for the sake of preserving for our own use, a venerable and sacred word—let us, I say, call the disembodied, or transembodied, or less cumbrously embodied gentlemen and ladies who study French and music in the spheres, and appear among us in celestial velvet and blue ribbons, (See Supernal Theology)—this is a very parenthetic and troublesome sentence—let us, I say, call these supernal persons—pneumatoid? psychoid? spiritoid? these would be proper and etymologically correct (except that the last is not very etymological) as indicating something spirit-like, or part spirit and part matter, but euphony will not permit the use of them—let us, then, I say, call these persons *spirital* people, and the new development, the *spirital* development, or *spiritism*.)—now, however, our modern Epicureans, Epicurean pro tanto, such has been their " progress," have discovered that man has no relations different in kind from those of a tree or an animal, (Great Harmonia Vol. ii. p. 230) or, as I should say, *another* animal, and of course, no responsibilities different from those of another animal. Both alike are under, and responsible to, the laws of Nature which are the *involuntary attributes of the deity, as the blood circulates without voli-*

tion. (The Present Age & Inner Life, p. 29) Now it is plainly inconceivable that a tree, or an animal, though they may be *evil* or *good* in a certain sense, should have *spiritual* relations, and responsibilities, according to the old meaning of the word, even so it is impossible that the *spirital* people, whether in the first or any other sphere, where their involuntary god *circulates*, should have such; hence, with praiseworthy consistency, that "jewel," they have all ceased,—the most flagitious among them included,—to be *wicked*, and are simply unfortunate, like a tree in a poor soil, or undeveloped, like a lean beast for want of provender ; not having come in contact with appropriate pabulum ; but having fallen rather upon old orthodoxy, and other dry crusts of conservatism, which bring leanness ;—hence, as I was saying, among the modern *evil* spirits there are no *wicked* ones ; that is, according to *spiritual* definition. But I was about to exhibit the *ancient* belief in regard to the character of the spirits.

"There are some who suppose that there is a certain obedient genus of dæmons, which is naturally fraudulent, omniform and various, and which assumes the appearance of gods and good dæmons, and *the souls of the deceased ;* and that through these everything which appears to be either good or evil is effected." (Porphyry to the Egyptian Anebo.)

Truly "there are some who suppose" identically the same thing at the present day, in order to account for identically the same effects. But the same author *asserts* that to be true which he says some *suppose.*

"By the contrary kind of dæmons all prestigious effects are produced. They constantly cause apparitions and spectral appearances, skilful by deceptions which excite amazement to impose upon men. *It is their very nature to lie ;* because they wish to be considered gods ; and the presiding power among them to be taken for the supreme god." (Porphyr. apud Eusebium.)

It must needs require great discrimination and knowledge of spirit character, one would think, to deal safely with such spirits as these. That this was, however, the real character of many of those in the habit of communicating with men, is acknowledged by still higher authority.

"Evil spirits, after a phantastic and fallacious method, simulate the presence of the gods and good demons, and therefore *command their worshippers to be just, in order that they themselves may seem to be good* like the gods. Since, however, they are by nature evil, they willingly induce evil when invoked to do so, and prompt us to evil. These are they who in the delivery of Oracles lie and deceive; and advise and accomplish base things. Moreover, the nature of evil dæmons is inconstant, unstable, inconsistent with itself, advising now one thing and now another." (Iamblichus, de abditis rerum causis.)

Now some of our own spirits are the exact apocatastatic counterpart of these, spiritists themselves being witnesses, (See Supernal Theology, & Spiritualism) *if they are not rather identically the same spirits*, and by what tests and criteria, Gentlemen Spiritists, are you to distinguish these from the honest guardian angels who inspire their *protegès* in a way "not much superior to their own mental development?" How do you know that they do not seem to obey your forms of adjuration, only that they may dupe you the more thoroughly? Do you not find that there is no safety, except in availing yourselves of the more mature experience of your apocatastatic predecessors? Cabbala, mystic, monosyllabic *spells*, amulets, talismans!—must you not return to these, as indeed you are doing? and then the Iamblichian method, which a man of more experience perhaps than all of you, found the only effectual one;—indeed why not send for Iamblichus himself? alas! how, in that case, to determine his identity? for spirits whose "very nature it is to lie" could not, I take it, be certainly relied upon, even if they should swear to it, by a spontaneous oath, as in the case of the identity of Swedenborg. How, then, are you to find your way out of such a labyrinth without the Ariadnean thread which you seem not to have hold of?—for, hear further one well acquainted with the intricacies of the place.

"Those who are themselves flagitious, and who leap, as it were, to things of a divine nature in an illegal and disorderly manner, *these* are not able to associate with the gods. Because, likewise, they are excluded through certain defilements, from an association with pure spirits, they become connected with evil spirits, and are filled from them with the worst kind of inspiration, are rendered depraved and unholy, * * * * * and, in short, become similar to the depraved demons, with whom they are consonant. These, therefore, attract to themselves through alliance depraved spirits &c." (Iamblichus de Mysteriis.)

It seems necessary to look well after the Mediums too, as well as the spirits, hence the ancients commonly selected the young and innocent for that office. The following curious quotation will also suggest another precaution very necessary to be remembered, while at the same time it exhibits the *insinuating* character of the *ancient* evil spirits.

"But an intellectual perception, above all things, separates whatever is contrary to the true purity of the phantastic spirit; for it attenuates this spirit in an occult and ineffable manner, and extends it to divinity. And when it becomes adapted to this exalted energy, it draws, by a certain affinity of nature, *a divine spirit*, into conjunction with the soul: as on the contrary, when it is so contracted and diminished by condensation, that it cannot fill the ventricles of the brain, which are the seats assigned to it by providence, then, nature not enduring a vacuum, *an evil spirit is insinuated in the place of one divine*. And what will not the soul suffer when assiduously *pressed* by such an execrable evil." (Synesius de Somniis.)

"Keep the head warm and the feet cool," lest the phantastic spirit be not sufficiently expanded to fill the ventricles of the brain!! The evil spirit, it seems, seeketh empty places! how admirably, and unexpectedly, this enables us to account for the haunted condition of certain heads and old houses! I am not aware that we have any apocatastatic parallel to *this* theory of possession. If not, it was not, perhaps, of the ancient sidereal semination, but only a dream of the author while discoursing on dreams.

But it is time to exhibit some of the opinions of those who held that all the spirits were evil.

" These impure spirits, dæmons, as is shown by the magicians, philosophers, and Plato, lurk about statues and consecrated images, and by their influence (afflatu) acquire the authority as of a present deity; one while inspiring soothsayers, at another making their abode in sacred places, sometimes animating the fibres of entrails, guiding the flight of birds, directing the lot, giving birth to oracles involved in many falsehoods; for they are both deceived, and deceive, since they are both ignorant of real truth, and keep back what they know, to their own perdition. Thus they gravitate downwards, and seduce from the true God towards matter, render life turbid, and sleep unquiet: *gliding secretly into the bodies of men, they simulate diseases*, terrify the mind, *distort the limbs, &c.*" (Minutius Felix, in Octavio.)

They could play pantomime, probably, and imitate the manners and peculiarities, even to the fits, and other diseases, of individuals, as the modern spirits are in the habit of doing.

" So also, they affect to be the authors of the things which they announce; and plainly they are of the *evil*, but of the good, *never*. They also pick out the purposes of God, sometimes from the mouths of the prophets, sometimes from the common interpretations of them. (lectionibus resonantibus.) Hence, also, gathering certain preordinations of events, they emulate divinity by stealing divine foreknowledge. But, in their oracles with what skill they can mingle equivocations, Crœsus can tell, or Pyrrhus." (Tertullian. Apologetic. c. 22.)

I shall be excused for quoting one or two, more modern opinions, which, however, seem to have been formed from an investigation of the ancient phenomena.

"You would say that the oracles were to be suspected, from the fact, that they were so ambiguous that an oracle was necessary in order to understand them. But, if the Oracles were the impostures of crafty men, it does not thence follow that they were not the work of illusive dæmons. I attribute them partly to both. Nor, if they were ambiguous, were they therefore not demoniacal; because the demons themselves, ignorant of future contingencies, relied upon subtile, but most often, fallacious conjecture. Wherefore the demons must needs use obscure and equivocal language, that it might be supposed the oracles were not correctly understood, if the event did not correspond to the prediction. Priestcraft is not a sufficient explanation, because many things were foretold beyond the reach of the human mind." (J. G. Vossius de Origine & Progressu. Idolatriæ.)

The following, for a Christian, is more like more modern, than it is like more ancient opinions than itself.

"There are some who suppose that certain subordinate spirits, partly good, and partly evil, instruments of retribution, observant of the things done here, traverse the air and earth; *who received from above a knowledge of things future, with the command to impart them to men;* sometimes in dreams; by the stars; by the Delphic tripod; by the entrails of immolated animals; and sometimes by a voice originating in the atmosphere, and then, as it were, diffused, and pervading the ears of men, which the ancients called "Divine Voice." * * * * * It will not be found that these things were unreal and futile, if one should attentively consider the subject." (Nicephor. Gregor. Histor. Lib. v.)

The author of the above is perhaps a little noncommittal in regard to his personal opinion of the character of the spirits. But let us return to more ancient sources. The following, from some of the "holy Fathers," are sufficiently explicit, but as they are somewhat peculiar, I must beg leave to quote the original language. These extracts are for the learned exclusively; ungrecian people, therefore, will please to pass them by.

Ιστορειται τοινυν περι της Πυθιας, οπερ δοκει των αλλων μαντειων λαμπρότερον τυγχανειν, οτι περικαθεζομενη το της Κασαλιας στομιον η του Απολλωνος προφητης δεχεται πνευμα δια των γυναικειων κολπων· του πληρωθεισα αποφθεγγεται τα νομιζομενα ειναι σεμνα και θεια μαντευματα. ορα δη δια τουτων, ει μη το του πνευματος εκεινου ακαθαρτον και βεβηλον εμφαινεται· μη δια μανων και αφανων πορων, και πολλω γυναικειων κολπων καθερωτερων, επεισιον τη ψυχη της θεσπιζουσης. αλλα δια τουτων, α ουδε θεμις ην τω σωφρονι και ανθρωπω βλεπειν, ουπω λεγεται η και απτεσθαι.

(*Origen. contra Celsum, lib. vii.*)

To the same purport speaks he of the "golden mouth;" and both he and Origen evidently express the opinions of others as well as their own.

Λεγεται δε η Πυθια γυνη τις ουσα, επικαθησθαι τω τριποδι ποτε του Απολλωνος διαιρουσα τα σκελη, ειθ' ουτω πνευμα πονηρον, κατωθεν αναδιδομενον, και δια γενετικων αυτης διαδυομενον μοριων, πληρουν την γυναικα της μανιας.

(*Chrysostom. Hom. xx.*)

I am not aware that the tripod, at least of the Delphic construction, has yet come into use among the modern Pythonesses.

But before dismissing this part of our subject, it may be well to ascertain the opinion of those who, anciently, held that there were both good and evil spirits, in regard to what kinds or classes of manifestations were due to the agency of *evil* spirits. The doctrine of Iamblichus was, evidently, quite different from that of the modern Expert, in regard to the effect of the mental development of the Medium upon the character or quality of the communication.

"It is necessary, however, to think that the soul which uses divination of this kind, not only becomes an auditor of the prediction, but also contributes in no small degree from itself to the consummation of it, and of what pertains to its operations. For this soul is co-excited and co-operates, and at the same time foreknows, through a certain necessary sympathy.

Such a mode, therefore, of divination as this *is entirely different from the divine and true mode*, being alone able to predict respecting *small and diurnal concerns*, viz: respecting such as being placed in a divided nature, are borne along about generation, and which impart motions from themselves to things that are able to receive them, and produce multiform passions in things which are naturally adapted to be copassive. Perfect knowledge however, can never be effected through passion. * * * but that which is mingled with the most irrational and dark nature of a corporeal-formed essence is filled with abundant ignorance." (Iamblichus de Mysteriis.)

He thinks also that the manifestations in, or by, those magnetized by music, *the enchanted*, which correspond almost exactly to a large proportion of modern Mediums, except in the method by which the "interior state" is induced,—these he thinks are all moonshine.

" Nor must you compare an ambiguous state, such as that which takes place between a sober condition of mind and extasy, with sacred visions of the gods, which are defined by one energy. But neither must you compare the most manifest surveys of the gods, with the *imaginations artificially procured by enchantment*. For the latter have neither the energy, nor the essence, nor the truth of the things that are seen, but extend mere phantasms as far as to appearance only."

" One may justly be astonished at the contrariety of opinions produced by admitting that the truth of divination is with enchanters."

" Nor must such truth be admitted as that which subsists between agents and patients, when they are concordantly homologous with each other." (have a common consciousness.)

The great disagreement of modern spirits on important points, and those too, such that they could not be misrepresented except wilfully, would excite the suspicions of Iamblichus.

" Nevertheless, no one of these is such as the divine species of divination ; nor must the one divine and unmingled form of it be characterised from the many phantasms which proceed from it into generation. (imitations) Nor if there are certain other false and deceitful resemblances, which are still more remote from reality, is it fit to adduce these in forming a judgment of it. But the divine form or species of divination is to be apprehended according to one intelligible and immutable truth : and the mutation which *subsists differently at different times, is to be rejected as unstable and unadapted to the gods.*" (Idem Ibidem.)

Truly, gentlemen Spiritists, there is danger, I think, that your spirit-intercourse will not, after all, prove to be apocatastatical of the true and venerable ancient theurgy ; but only of the damnably impious, and heretical ancient counterfeits of it, teste Iamblicho ipso, Experto longe omnium auctoritatissimo ; and so be found altogether the work of *evil* spirits, if not of such as it is proper to speak of only in Greek.

CHAPTER XI.

The description of paradise, which is promised unto the pious: therein are rivers of incorruptible water; and rivers of milk, the taste whereof changeth not; and rivers of wine, pleasant unto those who drink; and rivers of clarified honey; and therein shall they have plenty of all kinds of fruits. * * * * * They shall dwell in gardens of delight; reposing on couches adorned with gold and precious stones; and there shall accompany them fair damsels ("natural partners?") having large black eyes; resembling pearls hidden in their shells. MOHAMMED, KORAN. CC. xlvii. lvi.

THE JUDGE. I asked mentally, Where is he (Mohammed) now?

SPIRIT-BACON. Where he is I know not; but perhaps in the beautiful gardens he has so graphically described. SPIRITUALSM, SECTION xi.

There are several other resemblances between the ancient and the present spiritists, and their opinions and doings, which I will bring together in a miscellaneous chapter, under the head of—— as a merchant would say—sundries.

One of the most curious of these is the revival of the ancient "teletae," or service for the dead,—outside of the inclosure, I mean, by which it has hitherto been limited. The ancient pagans believed,—the spirits, doubtless, told them so, and the doctrine had been handed down from the "fertile period,"—that certain prayers and sacred rites helped the souls of the deceased; of those who died with any stain uncleansed upon them;—"that there are absolutions and purifications from sins through sacrifices, και παιδιας ηδονων, (funereal games, sports, *wakes?*) some for those who are yet alive, and some *for the dead ; those, namely which are called teletae, which deliver us from the sufferings there,*" (των εχει κακων, penal sufferings in the other world.) (Plato, de Republica Lib. ii.)

"But when one dissolves an injury committed by his father, by restoring, for instance, land which he had unjustly taken, he then makes himself to be unobnoxious to justice, and *lightens, and benefits the soul of his father.* * * * Hence the gods frequently predict to men that they should go to such or such places, and that an apology should be made to this man who was never known to them, and that he should be appeased, in order that thus they may obtain a remedy, and be liberated from their difficulties, and that the punishments inflicted on them by the Furies may cease. Thus, for instance, it is related of one who was cutting down an oak, and though he was called upon by a Nymph not to cut it down, yet persisted in felling it, that he was punished for so doing by the avenging Furies, till one who possessed the *telestic art* told him to raise an altar and sacrifice to this Nymph, for thus he would be liberated from his calamities."

The above is from a treatise of the Platonic Hermias, who, thus, as Mr. Thomas Taylor observes, " beautifully unfolds the meaning of the ancient indignation of the gods, through former guilt." Let us commend it, with other suchlike heathenisms to the next edition of The Conflict of the Ages.

The souls of the wicked anciently—for there were some wicked men *anciently.*—were punished in various ways, and for various purposes, and for various periods. Sometimes by penal pains in the other world, and sometimes by being sent back into this in a lower form than that in which they had sinned, as first in that of a woman, and then, if sin was still persisted in, in the form of a beast ; (Plato, Timaeus) a method not favorable to "progress" one would think. The punishment was in some cases temporary, and sometimes eternal. (de Republica Lib. x.)

The purpose of it sometimes the reformntion of the offender, and sometimes, *for the sake of justice*—if there is any modern consciousness correlative to that idea,—for the gods, anciently,—not being a mere involuntary circulating medium " as exhibited in the analogue of the blood flowing through the human body, unaided by *voluntary mental volition*"— the gods,—at least the good ones,—there will, however immediately arise a difference of opinion on that point,—the gods, anciently, insisted on justice being done ; punishing not only the sinners themselves in the other world, but their native places, their families, and children, for many generations, unless due restitution were made to the injured, or their heirs or assigns ; and due acknowledgement, and confession, and other appropriate recognition of the justice of their " ancient indignation " were offered to the gods themselves. But, oftentimes, those who had been sent back into this world by way of punishment for their sins while in it before, were still bound, such was the nature of the offence committed in the former life, to make these same *amendes honorables* to the gods, and they were afflicted by the avenging furies until they did it. Now here was a true difficulty, dignus vindice nodus, a knot, worthy of somebody who could untie it, for they had all been compelled to drink Lethe-water before they started on the second voyage of life,—or the third as the case might be,—and of course had not the slightest vestige of remembrance of what they were being punished for, did not even know that they were living a second life, and therefore could not take a hint of what the gods desired of them. These, then, were plainly, a class of cases for a good Medium. Accordingly, nothing was more common than for the public oracles, or private professors of the " telestic art," who could clairvoyantly see who such unlucky people had been, and what they had done in their previous life,—they could tell also who they themselves had been, and what they had done, as in the case of that every way thoroughly developed Medium, Apollonius Tyanensis, (See Vit. Apollon. Tyan.)—nothing was more common, I say, than for these *telestic* Mediums to point out to this class of sinners what crimes they had been guilty of, and what expiation the gods required further of them, whereupon, the due rites being performed, the hauntings and other annoyances ceased. (would this theory account well for some modern manifestations?) (See Plato, Proclus, Iamblichus, Hermias, and the Classics passim.)

Whether these same Mediums also informed the friends of souls suffering below and "asking prayers," what was to be done for them, and directed in regard to the "teletæ," I am not yet learned enough certainly to determine, but the analogical argument in favor of it would be, in this case, nearly or quite, equal to "the evidence of eye-witnesses."

Our apocatastatic parallelism here is very striking, that this ancient heathen service *for* the dead, should be re-evolved just now along with so many other fac-similes of the ancient spirit-times. It has not, however, come within the compass of my reading to find that the ancient spirits were as benevolently disposed, or rather, disposed to be benevolent on as large and liberal a scale as some of their modern successors. For instance, that Howard of a spirit who directed the apostolic circles in New York to pray nightly for the general jail-delivery and ascent to upper spheres of Hannibal and all his army. (See Supernal Theology.)

By the way, how wicked, beyond all recent parallel, must have been those old Numidian horsemen who so betrampled the Romans,—or else their souls must have been sadly neglected, —to lie in limbo all this time, while modern sinners "go up" in from three to twelve months.

Some of those too, who, in our time, descend, I beg pardon, begin to *ascend*, with all their sins upon their heads, unhouseled, unanneaied, are found to need, or to desire, deliverance from the εχει κακων, and solicit prayers, but whether they demand other due rites to be performed for them, such as restitution by their heirs, where extortion, and other unjust methods of gain were among their sins, which used to "lighten and benefit the souls" of rapacious sinners in the old spirit-times, I am not informed. However, the "evils there" have become so comparatively light and tolerable that I doubt whether any modern heirs would be in haste to remove them by such methods; for the Fiery Phlegethon flows now with nothing hotter than warm water just for bathing; the black Cocytus has become limpid; the bitter Acheron is a "sweet stream;" Tartarus is no longer much "murky;" and, in short, Elysium has spread pretty much all over Hades. These, it must be confessed, are apocatastatic resemblances with a difference, such however, is sometimes the effect of "Progress," although most people are apt to become rather worse than better by it.

It is much insisted on by the authors of, and believers in, the New Dispensation, that the consideration and belief that we are surrounded by, and in the presence of, spirits; and especially that our guardian angels constantly watch over us, and rejoice in our virtue, and grieve at our faults,—the old orthodox notion that we are ever in the presence of God, and that his eye is always upon us, not having been found of much avail,—cannot but have a very happy effect upon the manners and conduct of those who accept the doctrine. Such a doctrine too, cannot fail to afford, oftentimes, comfort and hope to those who need them, and strength and courage to the otherwise disheartened, by the suggestion that celestial good-will and spirit-aid are ever near us. I need not quote living, or spirit-authors, to exhibit this point,—I have promised to be brief—see spiritual periodicals, and other spirit- and spiritual literature, passim.

But it is interesting to observe the exact,—with the exception perhaps of what is said about dragging to judgment, which evidently savors a little too much of non-development, —and, I may say, beautiful apocatastatic coincidence of all this with the ancient views and doctrines upon the same subject.

"From this higher order of dæmons, Plato asserts there is appointed one to every individual as a witness and guardian in the conduct of life, who, though invisible, is always present a spectator not only of all our actions, but of every thought. But when life is finished, and we are to return, then he who presided over us, lays hold of, and, as it were, drags his charge to the judgment, and assists in the conduct of the case; if the soul attempts any falsehood, he contradicts it, if it speak truth he confirms it, and sentence is given very much according to his testimony.

Wherefore, all you who accept this divine doctrine of Plato as I have interpreted it, so conform your minds to it in whatever you do or think, as knowing that nothing whatever within or without the mind is hid from this watchful guardian, that with curious inquisition he comes to a knowledge of everything, that he sees everything, understands everything, that he dwells in your inmost souls, even as your own consciousness. He, of whom I speak, our especial guardian, peculiar governor, ever-present inspector, proper keeper, watchful observer, indivisible spectator, inseperable witness, disapprover of evil, approver of good; if he is rightly heeded, carefully consulted, religiously honored, is, for us, in uncertainty, a guide, in doubt, an adviser, in danger, a defender, in want, a helper, who is able, by dreams, by omens, and sometimes perhaps, if the occasion require it, by his visible presence, to avert evil, to promote the good, to elevate our fortune when low, to confirm it when unstable, to enlighten it when dark, to guide it when prosperous, to change it when adverse." (Apuleius de Deo Socratis.)

This is, certainly, what one may call an "Elegant Extract," or rather, eloquent extract, quite Jeremy Taylorish. I trust the spiritals will be grateful to me for it.

And the gods grant that they may profit by it, and try to rise a little above the boarding-school-Miss style when they next indite upon the same, or similar subjects.

The ancients were not all as dogmatic in regard to the doctrine of plenary inspiration as Iamblichus. Perhaps however, even he would admit that the *form* of the revelation might be somewhat modified by the character of the Medium, though not the matter of it. Some of the ancients, however, as is evident from the quotation already made from Porphyry, supposed the communication to be a sort of mixture or compound, or combination, derived partly from the spirit and partly from the Medium. Such also seems to be the opinion of many at the present time. I think, however, that the prevailing modern opinion is pretty apocatastatic of the following (certainly some such opinion is very indispensable in order to account for the *form* of the celestial *matter* in modern responses,) which I judge was the most common ancient opinion also, though different from that of Iamblichus perhaps in one direction ; and from that of the modern Expert in the other.

"If the verses of the Pythia are inferior to those of Homer, we need not suppose that Apollo is the author of them. He merely gives the impulse whereby each (prophetess) is moved according to her peculiar disposition. For if the responses were to be given by writing instead of speaking, I do not think the letters (γραμματα) supposed to be written by the god would be found fault with because they lacked the calligraphy of royal epistles ;—for neither the voice, the intonation, the diction, or the metre, is the god's but the woman's. He only causes visions, and supplies light to the soul in relation to the future." (Plutarch. de Pyth. Oraculis.)

This is plausible and convenient, as present similar explanations are of similar facts, and yet it seems to the uninitiated difficult to understand why Phoebus Apollo, or Benj. Franklin, or any other high celestial dignitary could not, or cannot, inspire the words as well as the thoughts, in so far at least, that the quality of the communication should not be deteriorated by its transmission through the Medium. And such, indeed, was the ancient theory in regard to responses from all *good* spirits. The ancients, it is true, held that communications from very high spirit-sources must pass thro' several Mediums and descend gradatim in order to reach "this terrene abode and the last of things." Apollo himself was only one of Jupiter's Mediums.

ταυτα γαρ πατηρ
Ζευς εγκαθιει Λοξια θεσπισματα.

"These oracular responses hath Jupiter commmunicated to Apollo."

Quæ Phœbo pater omnipotens, mihi Phœbus Apollo
Prædixit, vobis Furiarum ego maxima pando. (*Virgil.*)

"What things the omnipotent father hath foretold to Apollo, and Phœbus Apollo to me, those I, the Princess of the Furies, make known to you." But then anciently the Medium, whether remote, or proximate, was a mere conduit in relation to the *matter* of the message and did not absorb in its passage all the best of it, so that when it arrived at its destination there was nothing left "much above the mental development of the Medium." The spirit-Medium, however, if Medium he were, next preceding the human one, was often pretty high in rank and quality. Apollo, for instance, was one of the Dii Majores, and he seems not to have had any intermediate attorney between himself and the Pythia, because he often spoke in the first person, "I Phœbus Apollo." Even Jupiter himself, the father of gods and men, though he declined to honor any mortal man so far as to speak by his voice, yet condescended to nod, or *tip*, the head of his simulacrum in response to *men*, as he did his real head in reply to the *gods*.

Η, και κυανεησιν επ' οφρυσι νευσε Κρονιων.
* * * μεγαν δ' ελελιξεν Ολυμπον.

He spake, and bent his azure brow,
    Olympus trembled at his nod.

In modern times all these things are arranged somemhat differently, so much so indeed, as almost to endanger the apocatastatic parallel, as follows : " It is therefore, an unwarrantable thing to look for perfect wisdom, or for instruction much above the mental development of the Medium, because when the whole field is carefully examined it will be found that persons in this world do not, as they suppose, communicate promiscuously with Swedenborg. Washington, and other illustrious minds, *but always immediately with their own particular and congenial guardian spirit.* If the higher spirits desire to impart thoughts they do so by attorney. A long chain of "mediums" is at times formed between some exalted mind in the next sphere and a person on the footstool—but the spirit in closest sympathy with the earthly mind, is its own congenial protector. For an illustration, and I may add, a *fulfilment* of this law, the reader is referred to the preceding volume, page fifty-seven, where may be found this sentence : " A high society of angels desire, *through the agency of another and more inferior society*, to communicate in various ways to earth's inhabitants." Here you perceive spiritual media are acknowledged to exist as well as terrestrial channels,—the immediate spirit being, in almost every instance, the guardian of the person communicating. If these laws of interpretation be accepted, together with much to be hereafter said, the reader will find no difficulty in extricating his mind from doubts, arising from contradictions."

Shade of "the divine Iamblichus ! !" didst thou not appear in person to assure this weak and all incautious brother who could pen such inconsiderate babble, that such contradictory doings are altogether and indubitably the deeds of evil dæmons ? Truly, in another direction he shows himself cautious and clever, and has thrown out an anchor to windward against the storms of doubt and cavil, which if it had good bottom, would enable his ship to ride out the gale in gallant style ; meanwhile he has forgotten to look to leeward at the mocking spirits towards which his anchor drags rapidly, and which the ancient lighthouses make manifestly visible to all whose eyes are turned in that direction,—"*will find no difficulty in extricating his mind from doubts arising from contradictions!!*" forsooth? Alas! unhappy soothsayer, "who utterest things unworthy of Phœbus," thou art plainly in need of exorcism, for, listen to the highest known authority on this point: " *An evil demon requires that his worshiper should be just, because he assumes the appearance of one belonging to the divine genus,* (how easily you have been taken in by a little affected milk-and-water morality,) but he is subservient to what is unjust because he is depraved. The same thing likewise, that is said of good and evil *may be asserted of the true and the false.* * * * * * And that indeed, which consents and accords with itself, and always subsists with invariable sameness, pertains to more excellent natures; (is true and good) *but that which is hostile to itself, which is discordant, and never the same, is the peculiarity in the* MOST EMINENT DEGREE *of* DEMONIACAL DISSENSION, (falsehood of evil demons) *about which it is not at all wonderful that things of an opposing nature should subsist*" (Iamblichus de Mysteriis.)

Out of his own mouth he demonstrates himself and his compeers to be apocatastatic, much less of the true " mystic operators " of the ancient " telestic art " than of the profane enchanters and magicians, through whom the Roman politicians consulted the dead with such annoyance to the State, that they were driven forth on pain of death by decree of the Senate. (Tacitus, Annal. ii. 32.)

Another remarkable re-emergence from below the horizon, along with the rest of the apocatastatic curiosities, is that of the ancient heathen Elysium, in good preservation as any of the lately unearthed flying bulls of Nineveh. A gorgeous and glorious Paradise, where men shall enjoy freely and fully, aesthetic or sensuous pleasures, the same in kind as those which most of them can compass only partially and imperfectly in this world, and, oh, unconscious and admirable consistency! they take their pet dogs and horses along with them. Instead of saying "to-morrow shall be as this day and much more abundant;" their doctrine is that the next world shall be precisely like this, only a great deal better of the same sort.

"The gods shall send you to the Elysian plain, and the extreme margin of the Earth, where men lead facile, joyous lives. No snow is there, or wintry cold, or storms of rain; but Ocean evermore sends music-breathing zephyrs to refresh those who dwell there." (Odyss. iv. 563.)

"These happy heroes dwell devoid of care, by the deep-eddying Ocean, in the Islands of the blest, where thrice each year the bounteous Earth pours forth for them delicious fruits." (Hesiod, Op. & Dies.)

"They came at length to delightful regions, and charming verdant places, amid happy groves the seats of the blest.— Here the more widely expanded æther robes the plains in purple light, they have also their own sun and their own stars. Some on the grassy sward exercise their limbs, emulous, in various games, or wrestle on the yellow sand. Some perform the choral dance, chanting, while they beat the earth with their feet. * * * Here dwell the mighty heroes, born in better ('prolific') periods, Ilus, Assaracus, and Dardanus founder of Troy. At distance he admired their shadowy chariots, their javelins stood fixed in the earth, and everywhere at will their unharnessed steeds cropt the grassy meadows. *Such pleasure in their arms and chariots, such care to feed their shining war-horses, as they had in life, the same they feel in their present abode.* To the right and left he beheld them pic-nicing (vescentes) on the grass, and chanting in chorus a joyous paean, in the fragrant laurel-wood, whence through the forest flows the Eridanus with full stream. Here are those who fell fighting for their country; Priests, who, while life remained, *broke not their vow of chastity;* pious soothsayers, who *uttered things worthy of Phœbus;*

those who, by arts invented, rendered their life illustrious, and by deserving it attained to fame; all these, their temples bound with show-white chaplets, associate, and dwell together, here." (Virgil. Aeneid. vi. 638-665.)

The geography of the Elysian regions seems not to have been very well settled anciently. Some placed them upon the far-off margin of the Earth, some beyond the margin in the Islands of Ocean, some made them a part of Hades under the earth. Some others however, placed them in the milky way and ultimately still higher up, for the ancients also had their " Progress " from sphere to sphere, of which the present is not yet quite apocatastatic but becoming so in various respects, and especially by the reappearance of the doctrine of the pre-existence of the soul and of its descent with sins upon its head unto this "terrene abode." (See The Conflict of Ages, Spiritualism, Celestial Telegraph, &c.) Anciently the pre-existent soul descended from still higher regions into the milky way, where, according to Pythagoras, it first began to smell matter. "Hence he asserts that the nutriment of milk is first offered to infants because their first motion commences from the galaxy, when they begin to fall into terrene bodies." From thence the soul descended through various spheres to Saturn, Mercury, the Moon, &c., and after its trial in the body it gradually re-ascended if it were worthy, or if not, after repeated disciplines in the body, (unless it proved an incorrigible sinner) to its ancient blissful seats. (Macrobius in Somno Scipionis, Synesius, de Somniis, Plato in Timæo, & de Repub. x.)

It seems to have been a pleasant journey " through meadows of Asphodel," ("which were probably situated in the Lion" says Mr. Thomas Taylor,) and other amenities, both ways; so that it must have been, on the whole, an agreeable method of spending one's *eternity*, that journeying up and down,— analogous to that in which genteel people spend their *time*— especially, as, by the aid of Lethe-water, the "views," and other "lions," including the "meadows of Asphodel," "probably in the Lion," were of course, always as good as new.

The whereabouts of the modern, or apocatastatic paradise, one would think, ought to be somewhat more "definitely determined" than that of the ancient Elysium; inasmuch as the application of magnetism is now made, freely, not only to terrestrial, but to celestlal navigation also; nevertheless it is, evidently, about as hard to find as it used to be; however, it is undoubtedly in the same place, since it is prscisely the same sort of place, that it was anciently.

The following is pretty precise in its spherography and celestial statistics, and is authenticated by the fact that the Medium through whom it·was communicated was one which Swedenborg condescended often to visit, so that it may almost be considered as having the sign manual, or at least the signet of that sixth sphere dignitary attached to it. As the fact of his visiting the Medium is important, I shall first give the remarkable evidence of it. It seems he had announced his intended visit beforehand, as other great people do, and;

"On the occasion promised he came with some twenty spirits, all well known to us, and identified beyond a doubt. They all assured us of the fact, and voluntarily took an oath, declaring, "in the name of God," that Emmanuel Swedenborg was present." (Supernal Theology, viii.) This, then, may serve as a sort of credentials to what follows.

"The second (sphere) (the Earth being the first,) is above the atmosphere, about six miles in height. The third occupies about forty miles in height. The fourth occupies a still wider space, and so of the others, until the outer boundary of the sixth and commencement of the seventh, which is distant four or five thousand miles." (Idem xi.) "In rising to the spheres there are openings through which we rise." (Idem vii.) "As soon as I reached the sixth sphere I was conducted to my own home and left alone. I sank upon the grass and listened to the exquisite singing of the birds. * * * I felt as though I was just born into a most beautiful world. I went to my bed, which was made of roses, and laid myself upon it, and in a dreamy state of happiness fell asleep." (Idem, ibidem.) "I dressed myself and went into my garden. I saw all kinds of tempting fruit hanging upon the trees. * * * I took some of the fruit and eat it. It was the first time I had tasted *spiritual!* food. * * * There was a beautiful stream running through my garden. I went to the banks of it and there found a golden cup inscribed with my name. * * * When I rose to the seventh sphere I had but one guide who carried a lamp. * * * We have many parties in the spheres. At one of them in the sixth there were two or three thousand spirits present. We always dance and always have music. * * * I have a teacher in French, a teacher in drawing, and teachers in many other things. I have taken sketches of earthly scenes since I have been in the spheres." (Idem, ibidem.)

This is tolerably apocatastatic essentially, except that it lacks the dignity and good taste of Elysium, and except the locality, and except the learning French, which I fancy an old Greek could not easily be induced to take into his mouth. Pleasant places however, those spheres, for sentimental young ladies, with their "natural partners." (See Supernal Theology.)

But here comes still higher authority, perhaps the highest, or next to the highest. Loquitur the spirit of Swedenborg himself by the hand of Dr. Dexter.

"Now when I arrived at the sixth sphere * * * * the newness of everything impressed me with delight. The air was pure, and the whole heavens were clear and bright beyond all comparison. I saw no difference in the sky except in its brightness and purity; and on looking abroad on the earth I could detect no difference in its appearance from our earth, except in the heavenly beauty and harmony in the arrangement of the landscape. * * * The trees, the rocks and mountains, the flowers and birds, the gushing torrents and the murmuring rivulets, the oceans and rivers, man, woman and child all passed before me. * * * We occupy earth—tangible, positive earth—as much as your earth; but the advanced state of both spirit and locality renders it unnecessary for us to labor much to obtain food for the support of our bodies. Then again, the earth brings forth spontaneously most of the food required for our bodies. And * * * the advanced spirits do not require as much food as those who are below them."

In answer to a remark of the Judge in regard to locality and the probable difficulty of making an intelligible statement on that point, he said:

"I am glad your mind, Judge, recognises the difficulty of understanding locality in this connection. I might say Mars, or Jupiter, or Venus, but your mind would tire were I to lead it where the spirits of the sixth sphere dwell. I cannot locate it. Suffice it to say, far beyond the confines or limits of any star or planet of which you have knowledge." (Spiritualism, Section xv.)

This is quite satisfactory, and quite apocatastatic, except that Mr. Swedenborg has not yet arrived where dwell the ancient heroes, "for whom the bounteous earth thrice in each year pours forth delicious fruits," so that they are not obliged to work at all. He does not, however, agree with the previous witness, quasi accredited by himself, in the matter of locality; which seems to the undeveloped a little difficult to understand in regard to a mere geographical fact, and when both have been over the ground. If, for instance, of two earthly travellers, both of whom should assert that they had resided in London, one should inform us that it was in the East Indies, or beyond any place "of which we had knowledge," while the other located it in England or France, we should be apt to think that one of them, and possibly the other, had never been there. However, see the Present Age and Inner Life, page seventy-three; and yet, could not the spirit suggest or describe correctly, and the Medium's hand be a correct amanuensis for the description of one locality as well as another?

There is one more important witness on this point, viz., the "young Swedenborg," or apocatastatic Iamblichus, unless "the Judge" chooses to compete for this latter and higher honor—but whether to rank him before, or second to the last gentleman on the stand, I am dubious; for whether is more reliable, the *utterances* of a man who records the contents of his day-dreams as they *spontaneously* run throgh his head at something more than average speed, or the *expressions* of a spirit who, finding certain ventricles empty, (See Synesius, ut supra) "*insinuates*" itself into them, and being expanded by the warmth of the place, presses out, or *expresses* the braindribble of another man, who, meanwhile, is, himself, by the very laws of pathology in a *passive* state, for it is evidently a "case of compression" as the doctors say. But let us hear the witness.

"THE SPIRIT LAND!" What do you mean by these terms? Something *figurative*, or something literal? I mean a substantial world; a sphere, similar in constitution to this world, only, in every conceivable respect, *one degree superior* to the best planet in our solar system.

What is the external appearance of the Spirit Land?

It appears like a beautiful morning! The surface is diversified endlessly, with vallies, rivers, hills, mountains, and innumerable parks. These parks are particularly attractive. The ten thousand varieties of flowers lend a peculiar prismatic charm to the far-extending territories, and the soft divine ether in which the entire world is bathed supasses all conception.

Canst thou form an idea of the magnitude of the second sphere?

Multiply our earth by twenty-seven million times its present size, and it will give you the *exact size of one* of the countless parks of the second sphere.

How was the Spirit Land formed?

What law was it which formed the sparkling girdles of Saturn? What becomes of the fine invisible particles of matter which emanate from vegetation—from minerals, from all animal bodies, and from the *entire* globe? This earth alone gives off eight hundred millions of tons of invisible emanations every year. Where do *these* atoms go? The earth *perspires* like the human body. * * * * All the other planets—Mercury, Venus, the vast group of asteroids, Mars, Jupiter, Saturn, the three orbs beyond, together with all their *moons* —give off fine emanations just like the earth. Where do these emanations go? These questions are left you as replies to queré as to the formation of the Spirit Land.

Where is the Spirit Land located?

Seest thou that beautiful zone of worlds, at night, called the "Milky Way?" * * * Yon "Milky Way" is composed of myriads of suns and planets—each system resembling *our* sun with its planets. * * * * Our sun, our earth, and all the neighboring planets, constitute but one *group* in the circle. On these planets the *human spirit* FIRST begins to be. (Hence children drink milk, as Pythagoras says.) * * * Hence this circle of planets (taken altogether) may be termed "the first sphere of human existence." But the spirit of man at death passes away to *another* world; which is termed, very naturally, "the second sphere."

But where is this sphere located?

Look again at those *beautiful rings* surrounding the planet Saturn. * * * The second sphere girdles the first sphere, "the milky way," just as the rings girdle the planet Saturn. The representation is perfect." (The Present Age and Inner Life, pp. 273-6.)

There is not so much difficulty, after all, "Judge," in "understanding (or describing) locality in this connection," when once one becomes reasonably *clairvoyant*, and capable of going into the "Inner Life." The young Swedenborg is a much better geographer than the old one—such is the effect of "progress." But to understand "how the Spirit-Land was formed,"—truly, "hoc opus, hic labor est," equal to the hardest of the twelve which so illustrated the strength of

Hercules, "βιην Ηρακλεοιο;" this labor, however, how comparatively light;—to form, actually to *form*, the Spirit-Land, to evolve, and develop, the materials of it! Dii immortales! what a more than Thomsonian sweating operation it must have been for the poor toiling planets thus to provide for the souls of their children!!—to "*perspire* like the human body," to sweat out, a quantity of "fine invisible particles," or "insensible perspiration," which, when condensed into solid earth, and rocks, and trees, and rivers, and mountains, amounted to "*exactly*"—I beg pardon, there is a datum or two wanting here, such as the distance and thickness of the Saturn-like ring—but, say, to some ten hundred thousand million times the whole quantity of matter constituting the perspiring planets!!! truly, "Judge," here *is* a "difficulty," and I think I shall be obliged to confess that the labor of understanding is not less than that of doing it.

However, the parallelism between the ancient Elysium and the modern, notwithstanding some minor discrepancies, is, on the whole, and *essentially*, very striking and complete; that is, they are both essentially sensuous. Their relations are to the physiological, or at most to the psychical, to the spiritual in man not at all. In short they are what all *christian* men have ever, and what all *christian* consciousness ever will, denominate "a fool's paradise."

It is quite common for some persons, under the *New* Dispensation, to be at times *impelled*, that is moved by an impulse, in the physical sense, or certainly it comes very near to that, and in some cases quite,—they are urged and as it were, driven to go in certain directions without any conscious purpose, and without knowing in what direction they are to go, all of which is curiously coincident with such ancient facts as the following:—

"The effigy of the Heliopolitan god is carried about upon a litter, as the images of the gods are borne in procession at the Circensian games; and high priests, with shaven crowns, and pure by continued chastity, pass through the greater part of the Province ; and are borne along by a divine guidance, not by their own volition, whithersoever the god *propels* those who carry him ; as we see at Antium the statues of Fortune move forward in order to give responses." (Macrobius Saturnal. L. i. c. 23.)

The purpose of the god seems to have been, in this case, to peddle spiritual communications, a sort of traveling Medium for whoever might choose to consult him. In another similar instance of impulsion or propulsion, the god is represented as a sort of charioteer, (ηνιοχεων) guiding and urging those who bore him as a driver does his horses. And I have no doubt that, if the impressibles or propelables would now bear about with them "wrapt in pure linen," a duly consecrated image, or effigy, of their propulsive spirit—that, they would find the impulse, or propulsion, much stronger.

The ancients were in the habit also of inquiring after the spirits of their dead friends as at present. Thus, when Amelius inquired of Apollo in regard to the soul of Plotinus, the god gave response in a poem of nearly a hundred hexameters in his praise,—the philosopher seems to have been a favorite of his,—and setting forth that he was with Plato and Pythagoras and holy daemons, where they seem to have been in much higher, and more spiritual (not spirital) relations than those of any modern spirit ;—but then they were philosophers who despised matter, and body, and sense, even in this world. I would that the Judge, instead of putting faith in Swedenborg and the Pseudo-Bacon, could send for and consult *them* for a few sittings,—were they not so far up in "the intelligible," above the sphere of his sensuous, sight-seeing, apple-eating spirits, that they never could find them,—I think he would not fall as much below even the half-developed christian conscionsness in his record of spirital relations and employments, or in his theology, as he does now.

It was also the fashion anciently, as now, to make use of the spirits for very vulgar purposes, and to gratify very low or selfish ends.

"But by those who have devised the means of associating with beings more excellent than man, if the investigation of this subject is omitted, (viz: the path to felicity) wisdom will be professed by them in vain; as they will only disturb a divine intellect about the discovery of a fugitive slave, or the purchase of land, or about marriage, or merchandize: in this case, they will not be conversant either with gods or good dæmons, but with that dæmon who is called fraudulent; or, if this be not admitted, the whole will be the invention of men, and the fiction of a mortal nature." (Porphyry to the Egypt. Anebo.)

The ancient spirits, however, were somewhat more dignified than the modern in their language and manners, and physical manifestations;—true, that charioteering, or teaming the priests about, was a little earthly, and they were sometimes pretty noisy, and threw the furniture about *some*, in their own houses, as is the present fashion at their temple in Broadway; but to go into private dwellings, to slap people on the face, to creep into the pockets of venerable Judges, and knot up their handkerchiefs, to pull out young ladies' hair-combs, and play fantastic tricks with their dresses, (See Spiritualism, Introduction)—certainly, so far as I know, no ancient spirits were in the habit of doing such things.

Among the evidences, relied upon at present, of the spiritual origin of the manifestations, is the fact that the intelligence connected with them, asserts itself to be spiritual. The spirits also accredit each other's doctrines, and however contradictory they may be, (much more so than those of the ancient spirits) there is no difficulty in getting them attested and confirmed. So also the ancient spirits asserted their personality, and their knowledge of mens' thoughts, as, "I Phœbus," and "I know the thoughts within the dumb concealed;" and they also accredited each other, as where Apollo by an Oracle (See apud Euscbium,) sanctions the Egyptian, and other theurgy and Mysteries; and, in general, they seem to have been much more harmonious and concordant on most subjects than at present.

The parallel between the ancient heathen, and the prsesent spirit-intercourse might be extended farther by adducing more examples under most of the different heads, or by going more into detail in some respects. And, if, instead of relying, as we must, for the most part, upon incidental facts and allusions, scattered widely through ancient literature, the great number of ancient books, spoken of by their contemporaries, as written expressly on this subject, had come down to us, it would doubtless be easy to present it in a more full and orderly, if not scientific, form. For it is spoken of as a science by the ancients themselves, who assert that the knowledge obtained by it is certain and reliable in spite of all fraudulent daemons. However that may be, one thing is sufficiently obvious, viz : that the present form of it is quite crude and immature in comparison with its fullest ancient development.

Yet the similarity, indeed the identity of the two *in kind*, in fact, their true apocatastatic relation to each other, has been, I trust, demonstrated, and made certain, beyond all doubt, cavil, or evasion ; for what, I would inquire, except a return in large numbers of the "stars celestial, genitors of all events," to the same apocatastatic position, opening in some way the celestial avenues, could cause such a sudden and tumultuous re-descent of spirits, with the consequent repetition of the same phenomena as in ancient times?—as the same thick shower of meteors is repeated annually at the same season, that is, at an astral apocatastasis on a smaller scale.

CHAPTER XII.

It is all one as if they had said; * * * * * heathenry, paganisme, scurrillitie, and *divelrie itself* is equal with God's word; or that Sathan is equipollent with the Lord. PRYNNE. HISTRIO–MASTIX.

Quare, ut optimi medici conclamatis desperatisque corporibus non adhibent medentes manus, ne nihil profutura curatio doloribus spatia promulget; ita eos, quorum animæ vitiis imbutæ sunt, nec curari queunt medicina sapientiæ, eos mori præstat. APULEIUS DE HABITUD. Lib. ii.

As the best physicians do not, in hopeless cases, attempt a cure, lest they only prolong the sufferings of the patient; even so, those whose minds are contaminated with vicious opinions beyond the remedial power of truth, may as well be let alone.

Gentlemen Spiritists, you I mean who *willingly* believe in, extol and promote what you call the "*New* Dispensation," who believe that "the manifestations" are caused by the agency of spirits, not only, but, in the main, by that of *good* spirits, insomuch that you are thence enabled to make out a reliable description of the abodes and employments of the dead, and especially, to derive from their communications a true theology and religion,—this latter, far beyond comparison, or parallel, the most important and serious of all subjects, —I intended, when I commenced this present writing, after a little harmless apocatastatical preluding, a sort of light-aired voluntary, as some Church-Organs extemporize snatches of old love ditties, or fragments of war songs, before sermon, "for why should the Devil have all the good tunes?"—I intended, I say, out of a very serious subject, to make a very serious "Tract;" but my unfortunate—if such is the proper term—my unfortunate organization, education, associations, and other unpropitious surroundings,—for I was brought up among the "sects," and to reverence the Bible—these elements of my inner man coming into contact and combination with the spirital facts and spirital theories which have turned up to my investigation; the product has been such as quite to disperse my natural gravity, and have impelled me—should I not rather say *com*pelled me—to write, thus far, as I have written. I am not much in the habit of speaking with levity of any man's religion, erroneous though I may reckon it, yet in this case, I do not see that an apology is due, or fitting, even though, on sober second thought, I were conscious of impropriety or indecorum, which I am not,——certainly, an apology cannot without gross inconsistency be demanded, or expected by men who would persuade me that I have no responsibilities different *in kind* from those of a tree or an animal, that in all my relations I am, like the tree or the animal, wholly subject to the laws of Nature, and therefore must act as I am acted upon; men in whose theory "man is a part of Nature" whose philosophy, or theology, never ascends out of *nature*, never rises above the merely physiological, certainly not above the psychical, and never reaches at all the truly spiritual sphere of responsibility, and so gives no place, furnishes no ground, for an action which can justly or legitimately *owe* an apology,—for who would expect an apology from his horse or his dog, or his peach trees? Besides, this tract is not addressed to you, —with the exception of the present chapter, which is intented to be a serious one—nor written for your benefit, as indeed this chapter is not, although my benevolence would prompt me—excuse the egotism—to attempt to do you good, had I the slightest hope of being able to accomplish it, in regard to the subject under consideration. Yet I beg leave with all due respect both to you and to your spirit friends, to ask a few questions, and address a few remarks, to you, and to them if they choose, which, perchance may benefit some others.

You believe that communications true and valid are often made to you by the spirits of the dead, and that they often truly foretell future events, that is, that you have a veritable and reliable necromancy; (νεκρομαντεια) you believe that such communications as those, for instance, in the body of the late work called " Spiritualism;" were made by the celestially instructed, and thereby highly and deeply developed, and far progressed spirits of the men from whom they purport to come; also that the communications in the appendix of that work said to have been uttered by Webster and Clay through borrowed vocal organs, are the genuine productions and predictions of the spirits of those men; also that the spirit of the haughty and dignified Calhoun condescended to play fantastic tricks under the table, as there recorded. Your belief, gentlemen, in the true authenticity and genuineness of these communications—far m o r e wonderful, incomparably more incredible to me than any thing contained in that book —has gone far to convince me of the reality of spirit-influence,—for among all the facts of psychology with which I have become acquainted, judged of by whatever knowledge of the laws of mind I have been able to acquire—not altogether uninvestigating or unmeditative on such subjects— this belief of yours is by far—"far as from the centre thrice to the utmost pole"—the most extraordinary, the most unaccountable, by the vulgar and every-day laws of nature, and therefore the most demanding for its explanation the interposition of the gods or of some other spirits. However, you believe in these, and innumerable—numerous almost as the oracles of Apollo—other such-like phenomena, which you sometimes call the New Era, the new development, and more emphatically the "New Dispensation." I trust however, that you are satisfied it is not new in any essential particular; indeed, when it suits your purpose you can, and do, claim the authority of antiquity for it. Now if your spirit-theory rests on evidence which ought to command our credence, and your spirit-responses are reliable, much more, the ancient pagan spirit-theories and responses, by reason of longer continued, and more full evidence of the *same kind*, ought, in all logical minds, in point of proof and reliability, to take precedence of yours.

Are you then ready—and how should you not be, even as you value that "jewel" consistency?—with Mr. Thomas Taylor, to go over from Jehovah to Jupiter?—No, not from Jehovah, "the Jewish God is the creation of the nether portions of the brain," according to the Coryphæus of your quire; you have "progressed" far beyond *Him*—but from your great central germ, and involuntary circulating Medium of the universe, from your "Principle," and "identification of spirit with matter," are you ready to go over to Jupiter and Minerva, and worship the sun and the planets, and other Dii Majores et Minores? Truly, gentlemen, the difference is not great; it is but breaking the "Soul of the world" a little into fragments, a "disintegration" obvious, natural and necessary.

And why should not such magnificent combinations of the "Eternal Cause and the Eternal Effect" as are exhibited in the Sun, and Saturn, for instance, that "best planet in our solar system," be recognized and honored as divine as well as the sum total of such combinations? So did the ancients, only making practical your principles as well as their own. True, they personified more than you do; but were those philosophic men, with so much more science and experience in spirit-intercourse than you can pretend to, and with a power of analytic logic and intense thought which would put to shame you and all your spirits—were those men, who constantly held audible and visible intercourse with these very gods, (who probably knew as much about themselves as modern spirits) deceived in their deology, divology, or spiritology? And did not spirits of lower rank recognise and acknowledge the existence of these divinities, as yours do that of the presidents of the celestial phalansteries? If now these were all lying spirits, and these ancient believers were all duped by them—as you must confess, or else—for consistency *is* a jewel—adopt the attendant dogmata and ritual—with what face can you ask *us* to believe *your* spirits, who, judged by the ancient spirit-canons and tests, much more strict and scientific than yours, are all found to be "depraved and evil dæmons." Please, now, do not evade a fair question—were the ancients deceived in this matter of spirit-intercourse and spirit-teaching? if no, then recognise and obey the ancient teachings; if yes, then by what arguments are you to convince us that you are not dupes also? You will not however be persuaded, even by Mr. Thomas Taylor, to go over to Jupiter and Apollo, at least not at present, ultimately I think you will, for you already begin to talk of the "gods" and the "semidivine" in the spheres, but you are not *now* quite ready for the whole pagan divology and ritual, yet you have the ignorance or the effrontery to bring back, and offer to us as a new revelation, and substitute for Christianity, the dregs of the ethico-religious theories which belong to, and went along with, this pagan divology, and that too with the same sneers at Christianity with which your apocatastatic predecessors defended as better than it a higher form of these same theories. Do you believe that men not wholly ignorant of history will accept this pagan patchwork, which the spirits have fished up from the limbo of things lost, as something new and "never before vouchsafed to mortal man." Do you expect to resuscitate, wherewith to attack Christianity anew, this dead heathenism, which of old was suffocated and expired by the stench of its own noisomeness, so soon as Christianity could expose to the sun its fœtid corruptions and rottenness? do you think now to frighten Christianity from its propriety by raising the ghost of this dead champion? Surely, quem Deus vult perdere, prius dementat, as of old, or else how could you tolerate for a moment, how could you publish and annotate, how could you present to the consideration of rational men, such insane babble, such pantheistic nonsense, such a travestie of Democrito-epicurean day-dreams, such a "Vestiges of Creation" run mad, as is the Cosmogony of "Nature's Divine Revelations?" And yet, I know of nothing you have from the spirits, which, as compared with Christianity, is any more worthy of attention, or indeed, which is more reliable or better accredited—for is not the account of one who laying aside the body for a time, has visited the spheres, travelled through all time and space, and comes back to give their history and geography in his own person as worthy of acceptance as that of a spirit resident, who, as you yourselves say, can communicate what he knows only very imperfectly through the organs of another?

You and your spirits speak with bitter hatred, and with the most vulgar ribaldry of Christianity, and of all its friends; indeed, they and the legislators are the cause of most of the evils which exist among men—for, somehow, the development of the inherent *goodness* of the "disintegrated" fragment of the "great germ," which exists in *Man*, has been, always and everywhere, for the most part, and still is, repressed, or comes forth in the form of *evil*, through the *wickedness* of *men*—and yet, notwithstanding your instinctive, manifest, and palpable hatred of Christianity, you have the impudence to claim its Author as one of your Mediums, as did your heathen prototypes before you. You profess to look upon Christ as a man perfect beyond all modern example, hence a capital Medium, and one who, according to your theory, must have received his instructions and communications from the very highest sources; pray how do you reconcile it with the character of a man even of common honesty—if he was only what you and the spirits represent him to be—that he made such wholly false pretensions—as, that he came down from heaven, that he was before Abraham, that he would raise the dead and judge them, that he had all power in heaven and earth? Was all this only an oriental way of speaking, meaning that he was one of your preexistent germs, and that being a good Medium and Clairvoyant he thence derived the "knowledge which is power?" Moreover, deriving his doctrines—yourselves being judges—from the very fountain, or from a higher source than is possible for any other man, how is it that his essential teachings are so wholly subversive of your own? was his God the great Germ of Nature, the Soul of the World, an impersonal Principle, operating involuntarily throughout the vast machine,

"Whose Body Nature is, and God the Soul?"

a god towards whom it is impossible to be conscious of any moral or *spiritual* (in the christian sense) obligation, or indeed to hold any spiritual relations; for who would not be amused at the thought of spiritual responsibility to the law of gravity, for instance, or at the suggestion of his duty to offer gratitude, or religious homage, to that beneficent "Law of Nature," although in relation to him, and for him, it works out and exhibits, (at least in *spirital* language) Justice, Mercy, Wisdom, Truth, Love, Goodness? Is such the God whom Christ came to declare? And do his teachings express or imply the impossibility of the existence of *sin* in any spiritual sense? and does he accordingly apologise for it, as the unfortunate result of circumstances, and as deserving pity, and not punishment? and tell us that the wicked will be, in the next world, simply not quite as happy at first as others? —or rather, your doctrine is that—*not the wicked*, of which in your opinion, there *are*, and by your theory, there *can be*, none, but the "unprogressed," will be where some *others* might not be happy; but since they have their choice, and inasmuch as happiness is wholly a matter of taste, they can hardly be said to be less happy than others,—did Christ teach that the belief of religious truth is not an act of choice, and that therefore there is no obligation to believe what is not "mathematically demonstrated" to the understanding? and did he accordingly encourage men to ask for a sign, and to expect one to rise from the dead, as often as they had a doubtful question to be answered, or a morbid and profane curiosity to be gratified? Did he himself consult the psychometric Mediums around him, whose spirits cried out at his presence, "we know thee who thou art? Art thou come to torment us before the time?" Did Christ, while his mouth was filled with beautiful Epicurean aesthetico-ethical small talk, and Carlyleish sing-song of the "Eternal Laws," at the same time, dig down, and subvert, the very foundations of all spiritual righteousness and religion? Did *he* preach nothing beyond your merely zoological, or apiary virtues, and enforce or urge the practice of them by the promise of Mohamedan gardens, and other beautiful and most delightful paradises, for—Animals? Is it possible that *such* a substitute for Christianity can be deliberately offered, with sneers at "old mythological religions," by sane men, to a Christian people? or that any *Christian* man can contemplate it, without the mingled feelings of astonishment, grief, scorn, pity, and "righteous indignation," at so monstrous, and impious a proposition? With such an "improvement" upon Christianity, as I suppose you call it, or a "progressed" Christianity,—for some of you are very indignant at the suggestion of a doubt in regard to your being Christians; indeed, you condescendingly propose to reaffirm the fundamental truths of Christianity, "clarified from error,"—with such a dead heathenism, mingled with a maimed christianity, and that robbed of its vital principle, and cut off at the root, how dare you appeal to Christ as among those who confirm your doctrines? Well,—and truly, for once,—may your spirits inform you that they never have seen Christ, and you might perhaps learn from other quite as reliable sources, that, probably, they never will. You seem fond of appropriating the language of christians; everything with you is "*spiritual.*" Had you studied Christianity instead of vituperating it; had you "progressed" by the development of your own spiritual being, instead of talking so much of " Progression ;" you would, by this time, have discovered that your " New *Dispensation*," as you falsely and profanely call it, so far from being *spiritual*, never anywhere rises above the merely psychical, that it neither recognizes nor provides for—rather excludes from its very idea—truly *spiritual* relations.—However, it were idle to attempt to make you understand the christian definition of that word ; for how is it possible for you to apprehend that, which to know, requires the exercise of faculties still latent ? You appeal very triumphantly to your evidence of the mathematical certainty, and "*real reality*" of spirit-intercourse and spirit-responses. My purpose does not require me at all to dispute the fact . but do you not perceive that the " real reality," and *truth* of the said responses, in regard to things otherwise unknown, in regard, that is, to the new ("so called,") teachings of the *Dispensation*, do not thence, by any means, follow ? Do you not perceive—no, excuse me, you cannot, seeing perceive what is nevertheless true,—that for the christian consciousness no supposable quantity or degree of the evidence you speak of, accompanied by the doctrines you teach,—should your circles be seen daily, or nightly, floating and gyrating in the air, and chanting pæans in honor of their patron spirits ; should the said spirits personally appear, robed in the real Iamblichian halo, and by voluntary oath or affirmation, attest each others truth and veracity ;—should all this, and still more astonishing *new* developments of the laws of nature occur, it would only prove to the christian intellect and consciousness, the existence of a dæmonopathy of which falsehood is the natural product.

But, the tree is known by its fruit, and your healing Mediums, your possessed or obsessed people. as you assert them to be, restore the sick, and do undeniable cures. There is no occasion to doubt it. The ancient theurgists, and heathen Mediums also did the same, (see Vita Apollonii.) and even Roman Emperors, who are not usually reckoned a very pious class of men. (Tacitus) So also, does every *new* patent medicine, and *new* medical theory. It were an excellent stock in trade for a "Curiosity Shop," to fish up, from "the deep deep sea" of the past, but a tithe of the medical "infallibles" which lie buried there, and which infallibly cured thousands upon thousands in their time. Here is one as good, and as marvellous in its effects, as any of the spirit-recipes; —for why? it is also of *celestial* origin.

"*An admirable Oyntment for Wounds.*"

"Take of Moss that groweth upon a Scull, - - ii. oz.
Of Man's Grease, - - - - - - - - ii. oz.
Of Mummy, and Man's Blood, each, - - oz. ss.
Linseed Oyl, - - - - - - - - - ii. Drach.
Oyl of Roses, & Bole-Armoniack, each, - i. oz.

Let them be all beat together in a Morter so long, until they come to a most pure and subtil Oyntment; then keep it in a Box. And when any wound happens, dip a stick of wood in the blood that it may be bloody; which being dyed, thrust it quite into the aforesaid Oyntment, and leave it therein; afterwards binde up the wound with a new Linen Rowler, every morning washing it with the Patient's own urine; and it shall be healed, be it never so great, without any Plaister, or Pain. After this manner you may Cure any one that is wounded, though he be ten miles distant from you, if you have but his blood. It helpeth also other griefs, as the pain in the Teeth and other hurts, if you have a stick wet in the Blood, and thrust into the Oyntment, and there left. These are the wonderful gifts of God, given for the use and health of man." (*Paracelsus of Celestial Medicines.*)

There are other by-gone specifics, innumerable as the oracles of Apollo, equal to *this*, in mystic virtues; and let not any prudish recent Unguent stink contemptfully, or medical infidel sneer, or modern healing Medium turn up its nose,— for *these*, also, each in its time, could boast of undeniable and *undoubted* cures, at least, no one competent to form a correct opinion will be disposed to douht the reality of them. And yet, notwithstanding the "immutability of the laws of nature," and that "retrogression is an impossibility," in a short time, such things are no longer heard of, and sick men are fain to fall back into the hands of the disciples of Hippocrates, and under the vulgar and every-day laws of Nature. I was once cognizant of a new development on a small scale where the subjects of it were under the direction, not of the spirits, but of "the spirit." "The spirit" directed them to heal the sick which they did—in one case "the spirit" directed them to go to a woman who had been eight years bed-ridden, and to command her to arise and walk; they obediently did so, and the woman arose and walked. Thereupon "the spirit" feeling itself strong, commanded them to raise the dead, but on this occasion "the spirit" proved to have more courage than conduct. These people were wholly, in all their relations, under the direction of "the spirit," and were immaculately holy; but alas for divine and sinless human nature, "in unfortunate circumstances," "the spirit" directed brother B., to take brother F's wife, and brother C., to take Miss L., for their "*spiritual* partners," &c., &c., of which spiritual unions followed results much more physiological than spiritual. Thereupon this development—for bigotry and intolerance are not yet wholly eradicated from among men—was suppressed.

There is a principle as old as "the primitive history," or "excellent soft bark," as some of you call the Bible, reasserted by Christ, insisted upon most bigotedly, as you must think, by St. Paul, more modestly by other Apostles, reiterated in modern times especially by Pascal: to the effect that the miracle is to be judged of by the doctrine, and not the doctrine by the miracle. These are not red-letter names in your calender, and their opinions, I am aware, will not be authoritative with you, but, as I said before, this Chapter though addressed to you, is not written for you. What then are your doctrines? A pantheistic theology, the identification of God with Matter, or, a Soul of the World, or vital Principle of the Universe;—hence, man's responsibility is only to the Laws of Nature; the denial, consequently, of the fact of true spiritual relations, of the existence of sin and guilt, with an attempt to show that the universal consciousness of humanity on this point is fallacious and false;—the reiteration of the so often exploded falsehood, that man, having no *free will*, is but an involuntary and irresponsible link in the endless chain of Nature;—the reassertion, therefore, of the primal lie of Eden—" Ye shall not surely die;"—the physical demonstration, for as many as comprehend *interiorly* the immutable laws of Nature, of the immortality of the soul; because it is perfectly obvious from the "inherent and immutable laws of progression," that every particle of matter in the Universe ascending through multifarious forms, from the angular to the circular, from the circular to the spiral, and so on to the spiritual, " will ultimately pass to the perfection of a spiritual essence;"—allurement to virtue by the promise of delicious oriental paradises, after death, of which however the most vicious, as well as the virtuous, may take their choice in the spheres;——this linsy-woolsy tissue of ancient and modern sophistry, absurdity, and impiety, sugared over with sickly sentimentalism, and milk-and-water morality, with the privilege of perpetual appeal, for its true interpretation, to the re-established pagan oracles, and ancient necromancy revived; —this, Gentlemen Spiritists, *this!!* is your substitute for Christianity, *your* remedy for all the ills of humanity, your panacea for the diseases of society, your Grand Catholicon, Matchless Sanative, and Elixir Vitæ, for the regeneration, reorganization, and earthly perfection of mankind.

But these doctrines and principles seem not, at first sight, at least to ordinary minds, at all calculated to produce the effects promised from them, the specific not at all adapted to the disease. How then comes it that such magnificent results are so confidently predicted from the effect of such apparently inadequate causes? Why, plainly, just as in chemistry, the mixing of two fluids will sometims, most unexpectedly to the non-scientific observer,—and, indeed, to the scientific also, until after experiment,—produce a solid, or the rubbing together of two solids produce a fluid ; and as in medicine, the physician is astonished at first to find some of the most tasteless, and as he would think, inert, substances produce the most energetic effects ; even so, in moral pathology, remedies must be at first empirical; and here, especially, "foolish things," that is, things which one would not suspect to have any such latent virtues, are sometimes found, it is said, to prove most successful—by experiment. The old adage, "nemium ne crede colori" don't trust to appearances, is, no doubt, therefore, as true in morals as anywhere else. It is obvious then, gentlemen Spiritists, that your confidence in spiritism is not the result of any rash and incautious theorising, a conclusion drawn from ill-established premises, but that you have followed the true Baconian method, in short, that it is founded on experience. I had, for the moment, well nigh forgotten, that, among other apocatastatic coincidences, the very same doctrines which you teach, authenticated and confirmed by the very same methods, backed, and sustained by the same energetic development of the *understanding*, accompanied by the same scientific and commercial activities, practically applied, on the largest scale, to the same public improvements and facilities, and to the same æsthetic civilization ;—these same doctrines, aided by the same attendants and circumstances, were tried in their effects upon the morals of the communities of the ancient period, on a very large scale, and with very uniform results. Certainly, the trial was sufficiently long, and sufficiently varied, to be quite satisfactory. You have, therefore, I admit, an undeniable, and inalienable, right to appeal to experience against all gainsayers. And the result of that experiment,—how admirable ! ! Surely, you must admire it, and therefore you are so desirous to bring again into full operation the causes which produced it. The morals of old Rome the Mother of arms ! from the palace of the Cæsars, down to the ergastulum, and the *studies !* of the gladiators; the morals of Athens! the Mother of Arts!—the morals of Antioch! the seat of the politest ancient civilization, the Paris of antiquity,—the morals of Alexandria! the gate of ancient Commerce!—the ancient Republic, the Empire, in all their provinces,—how exempt from social and political depravities!—how free from the mis-organizations of society to which you attribute most modern misdemeanors!—how "progressed" almost to obedience to that Law of Association and Brotherhood which is your summum bonum for this world and the next! *This* morality, this legitimate and admirable result of ancient spiritism, how desirable that it should take the place of the modern tame, timid, moral prudery, "cabined, cribbed, confined," shorn of its fair proportions, and restrained of its "free development," by "the gloomy dogmas" of the "old mythological religion!" how desirable! how desirable!! and when, as the spirits triumphantly promise, faith in the New Dispensation shall have become "universal," then shall that (by you) devoutly wished for consummation be realized!—then shall our apocatastatic period have completed itself, and have come back, full circle, copying in detail, or rather, repeating, as the doctrines and "manifestations," so also, and consequently, the manners and morals, of its illustrious predecessor! alter et idem! alter et idem!!

CHAPTER XIII.

> The oracles are dumb,
> No voice or hideous hum
>   Runs through the arched roof in words deceiving,
> Apollo from his shrine
> Can no more divine,
>   With hollow shriek the steep of Delphos leaving.
> *   *   *   *   *
> Peor and Baalim
> Forsake their temples dim,
>   With that twice battered god of Palestine;
> And mooned Ashtaroth,
> Heavens queen and mother both,
>   Now sits not girt with tapers' holy shine.
> MILTON, ODE ON THE NATIVITY.

> Ὁ μεγας Παν τεθνηκεν.
> The great Pan is dead.
> PLUTARCH, DE ORACULORUM DEFECTU.

What is the true and natural relation of Christianity to the present manifestations? In order to answer this question correctly it seems to me necessary first to inquire in regard to the character of the ancient δαιμονιζομενοι or demoniacs spoken of in the New Testament. Were they persons laboring under certain diseases supposed to have been induced by the presence or agency of malignant dæmons; or were they those whose organs were taken possession of and controlled by spirits, in the opinion of persons of that period, in the same manner as spirits are supposed to control and act through the organs of certain persons at the present time? It is plain, I think, from the New Testament, that it was not the common opinion at that time, as some have asserted it was, that diseases in general were produced by some agency of evil spirits, because the distinction is everywhere made between "healing diseases," and "casting out devils." Neither does it appear that any *particular* diseases were supposed to imply, necessarily, the presence of spirits. The most that can be inferred from the New Testament is that diseases did not exclude them. Certain diseases are commonly supposed to have indicated to the ancients the presence of dæmons—insanity, for instance; yet this disease is spoken of as being cured in the New Testament without any mention of dæmons, although in another place a lunatic is mentioned as being also dæmoniac. So dæmoniacs are spoken of who were deaf and blind, but deafness and blindness are cured also where there were no dæmons. Epilepsy is one of the diseases which it is thought the ancients believed to be owing to spirit agency; and the case in the New Testament where the possessed is said to have been thrown down, and "wallowed foaming," is often reckoned a case of epilepsy. It is certain, however, from ancient profane authors, that epilepsy often occurred where there was no suspicion of dæmons; it is also in evidence that in some kinds of possession the person supposed to be under control of the spirits fell down and foamed at the mouth. Thus in Apuleius (Oratio de Magia) it appears that he was accused of enchanting a certain boy, because he (the boy) exhibited symptoms of epilepsy in his presence; but he was acquitted by proving that the boy had *real* epilepsy, and that there was therefore no occasion to suppose enchantment, or the induction or presence of spirits. The Pythia, too, was convulsed and foamed at the mouth, and so, probably, did all those who were said to divine by "*rage and fury.*" I think the conclusion is legitimate, therefore, as far as regards the New Testament, that the δαιμονιζομενοι are not to be considered as, in the opinion of their contemporaries, merely diseased persons. It seems certain, then, that they were supposed to be persons possessed and controlled by spirits in such wise that their organs during the obsession did not respond to their own volition but to the will of the dæmon; for it is evident that the phenomena were not looked upon as owing to any merely abnormal condition of their own minds, but to the presence and agency of some other intelligent and personal beings. That such was the opinion is plain from the history, because the possessed persons are not said to act or to speak, but the *spirits* are represented as the agents in all that they do or say. Their object then, plainly, was not to inflict disease of body or mind, any more than it is of their successors at the present time. They seem to have been no more numerous, propably less so than at present. In the whole of Christ's ministry there are not recorded, perhaps, more than a dozen instances of the exercise of his power to cast them out, though sometimes more than one, and sometimes many persons may have been set free where only one record is made.

They seem to have acted through—as we should say—Mediums of different kinds. Most of the possessed, or at least many of them, were evidently very good speaking Mediums— the spirits spoke by them readily and rapidly. Several, however, are recorded as dumb, where it is remarkable that the spirit and not the man is said to be dumb, that is, he had not yet acquired control of the Medium's organs of voice. Others appear to have been Mediums for the physical manifestations, perhaps for pantomime, as where the dæmoniac simulated epilepsy; and the spirits of the dæmoniacs among the tombs could both speak, and exhibit as much physical energy as the strongest of the modern spirits. Other persons again were simply *troubled* (ὀχλούμενοι, disturbed, vexed) with evil spirits —they were perhaps rapping about them, seizing them by the arm, scratching them on the legs, patting them on the head, and after other modern methods soliciting leave to enter, or perhaps they were noisy about their houses, deranged their furniture, &c. These Mediums too, like other ancient Mediums, as the Pythia, the Indian Sages, and Apollonius Tyanensis, and like many modern Mediums also, seem to have been clairvoyant, or psychometric, that is, they could read the characters of those they looked upon, for they cried out at the presence of Christ, " we know thee who thou art ;" so also the soothsaying damsel spoken of in the Acts exclaimed at sight of the Apostles, " These be the servants of the most high God."

It does not appear definitely from the Evangelists whether these dæmoniacs made any use of their peculiar s*pirital* endowment, or the spirits of *them*. They are spoken of incidentally, just as we now speak of Mediums, it being taken for granted in either case that everybody knows what a dæmoniac or a Medium is. The case however in the Acts, which is perhaps the key to many of the others, answers precisely to one of our female Mediums travelling with her keepers for their mutual benefit, and it is evident from other sources of information that the heathen world at that time was full of such, and they were probably not wanting in Judæa.

These ancient dæmoniacs were, then, undoubtedly parallel, and the same in kind, with those persons who claim the honor of being considered the subjects of a similar dæmonopathy at the present time. That dæmoniacs were common among the pagans as well as the Jews is proved by the Acts of the Apostles and also by profane authors; and since *they* are known to have been Mediums for divination and other purposes, the conclusion seems unavoidable that those among the Jews were also connected more or less with the divination and necromancy of the period. The character of the sorcerer, too, at Samaria, seems to have been identical with that of the magicians or enchanters scattered throughout the Roman Empire, by whose aid people were in the habit of consulting the spirits. And there was plainly no difference *in kind* between the spirit manifestations spoken of in the New Testament and

those so common in the heathen world at the same time.—
Now it is not necessary to my purpose to determine the point, or even to express an opinion, whether the ancient spirit-phenomena as they were by some at that time supposed to be, occuring both among Jews and pagans, were really produced by the agency of unearthly spirits, or if they were not rather the effect of certain relations of the human mind and body the law of which was at that time, and is now, unknown. This point, in regard to the facts recorded in the New Testament, will be decided, probably, somewhat according to the inquirer's answer to the previous question, "What think ye of Christ?" Those who attribute to him the highest character, must of course believe that the true explanation was perfectly well known to him. If then the phenomena were not at all the effect of spirit-agency, it is extremely difficult, to find a reason why he spoke and acted in accordance with the common but erroneous view of the subject taken by his contemporaries. That there may have been reasons sufficient to induce this line of conduct cannot be denied, but at the same time, they must, I think, be unknown to men. Those for whom his opinion would not be authoritative would of course determine their own on other grounds. I think it cannot be gainsayed, however, without a pretty violent interpretation of the New Testament, that both Christ and the Apostles believed the manifestations which come under their observation, to be owing to the presence of spirits. But whatever may be the decision of this point, I think it is certain beyond all honest doubt, that the whole ancient dæmonopathy, if dæmonopathy it were, including both Jews and pagans, with all its attendant manifestations, was essentially the same thing in kind, and the product of essentially the same causes as what is now technically called the "New Dispensation"—that the present spirit-phenomena and spirit-intercourse are but the reiteration of the same things which, in ancient times, were at their height about the commencement of the christian era. What then was the aspect of christianity, and of its friends,

towards this development at that time? Did the conduct of Christ indicate that he thought it offered—whatever might be his opinion of the cause of it—a legitimate method of holding intercourse with the dead, and of acquiring information in regard to the future world? Some of the spirits whom he met with were evidently not altogether uninformed in regard to the "spirit world;" was he in the habit of consulting them on that point or any other? Did Paul request the soothsaying damsel or her keepers to put him in communication with the spirits, that he might inquire in regard to the proper doctrine to be preached? or did Peter ask Simon Magus to enchant some boy for him that he might have his curiosity gratified in regard to the geography of the many mansions which his Master had informed him of the existence of? Did the Apostles advise or encourage ειδωλολατρεια, or the practice of frequenting and consulting consecrated images, by which responses were given, and spirit-intercourse carried on, as it is now by tables and other furniture?

Did Christ or the Apostles encourage the kind of curiosity which is stimulated and gratified by the present, as it was, by the ancient necromancy? Was there, in his opinion, no obligation to recognize and obey the spiritual truth which he taught or any spiritual truth, unless it was authenticated by that kind of evidence? Did St. Paul reckon the pagan spirits to be the far progressed, highly developed, and "semi-divine" souls of dead men, whom it would be highly proper to consult in regard to theological matters, when he wrote the first chapter of Romans for instance, or when he said that the heathen offerings were made unto devils? Does the New, or the Old Testament anywhere advise *necromancy* as the true art or *science* whereby to arrive at a correct knowledge of the world to come?

Certainly whoever considers these questions with an examination of the opinions of the Founder, and of the first promulgators of Christianity, cannot fail of the proper answer. But men often have incorrect opinions, alas! how often, —of what is implied in their own principles. Did these men, then, misunderstand their own doctrines in this respect, and is it appropriate and necessary for Christianity, that "one should rise from the dead in order to convince us that its principles are not delusive and false? or to enlighten us where its principles come short? Does it teach anything which does not find its correlative consciousness, and recognition of its truth, in every human soul, which does not love darkness and neglect or refuse to bring itself into conscious relation to the whole truth which it teaches? Can any human soul ask any question in regard to the true principles of *duty*, in regard to its true *spiritual relations*, in regard to what constitutes the *true well being* of the human spirit, in regard to the means necessary to attain *that highest end*, which Christianity does not answer? Or is this not the proper purpose of religion? which ought rather to address itself to the senses and sensuous understanding; and to "consider its teachings on the *habits*, life, condition, and *circumstances*, of the spirit after death of the most vital importance properly to be communicated;" (Spiritualism, p. 134) and so, to gratify idle curiosity, and make the sensuous, and even the sensual *happy*, by describing to them as their future residence, celestial gardens most delightful to the senses, where they are to meet their wives and children and cousins; and by assuring them, with testimony of those risen or returned from the dead, who have been there, that "*spiritual food!!!* (Supernal Theology) consists of more delicious apples and peaches, and other fine fruits, had with very little labor, than inhabitants of *this* Earth can have any conception of? Is this, after all what is *implied* in, a sort of appendix to Christianity, a "progressed" Christianity, notwithstanding the *opinions* of its Author, and which therefore very legitimately appeals to necromancy as among its appropriate, and most satisfactory evidences? Christ and Christianity forgive me for asking the question.

It is plain that Christianity is, in its principles, at irreconcilable hostility with this re-development, and resurrection of the old spiritism, as it was at first with all the ancient forms of it. Indeed, at its very advent, it declared war against it; in its very cradle it strangled this serpent; or, rather, "bruised the heads" of this Hydra, and even amputated them. However, it is in their very nature to sprout again—not now for the first time—as soon as the cautery of pure undiluted spiritual truth ceases to be applied to them. True, they do not now appear—not yet—as Jupiter, and Apollo, and Venus, but they are the heads of the same beast still. Pan, indeed, "the great Pan," who was announced as dead, with groans and wailing of "the spirits," is fully resuscitated in his ancient form and proportions, which accounts well and naturally, for the reappearance of so many Satyrs in our time.

What then should be the aspect of Christianity towards the present manifestations? It is not for me to advise the Church. Yet surely, one would think,—were she wise in her generation—that she has tried sufficiently the experiment of descending from her proper sphere of the spiritual; of meeting the world half-way, or some other proportion of the way between them; of borrowing the weapons of her foes; of subsidizing her natural enemies to fight in her cause. The Church, however, even the most unspiritual and semi-worldly organizations which go by that name,—with the exception perhaps, of the extreme *left* wing of the universalists—is not, I think, in danger of any coalition or coalescence with the present self-confident and very *threatening* development. Its materialism is too gross, its sensuousness too coarse, its Deity, if Deity it has, too Epicurean, its attacks upon Christianity too unskilful and vulgar, to seduce *permanently* more than the merest vestibulary lodgers in the Church; or to alarm more than a few of the most timid worldly-wise-men. To "the world," whether in the Church, or out of it, it seems likely to become a more than ordinarily dangerous form of delusion; yet even in "the world," where it can be brought, in its true and full lineaments, to the perception and consciousness of men, I trust that few except those—perhaps not few—who are pre-adapted and pre-conformed to it, will remain long under its influence.

CHAPTER XIV.

> Almyghte God that made mankyn,
> He schilde his servandes out of syn,
> And maynteyne tham with might and mayne.
> METRICAL ROMANCES.

> For never wight so evill did or thought,
> But would some rightfull cause pretend, though rightly nought.
> SPENSER, FAERIE QUEENE.

> Much pains have been taken to poison the minds of all ranks of people, but especially the middling and the lower classes, by the most impious and blasphemous publications that ever disgraced any Christian country.—PORTEUS.

In this concluding chapter I wish to address a few words to believers in Christianity. Not indeed to those who are fully and in the highest sense Christians. They, having found the words of Christ more than verified, that he who comes to Him shall never hunger, and that he who believes on Him shall never thirst, need not, neither would I presume to offer to *them* any suggestions in regard to the subject under consideration. With whatever kind, or degree, or amount of evidence the "New Dispensation" should be offered to their spiritual perception, it would be instantly and indignantly rejected by the inherent antipathies of the spiritual life. But there is another, and much larger class of Christians, many of them, indeed, only nominally such, who, although their moral sensibilities are shocked, become puzzled and bewildered by the "manifestations," so strange, marvellous, and as they suppose, altogether new; and so are induced to admit the truth of the theory of spirit-agency because they see not how else the facts are to be accounted for. Having gone so far, another and wholly different conclusion, viz., that such a wonderful and unheard of intervention of departed spirits can be only for most important and *truthful* purposes—this second conclusion I say, is, as it were, smuggled in, under cloak and cover of the first, although they are entirely distinct, *and have no natural or necessary connexion.* Indeed, in regard to the first conclusion, they do not seem to remember that, although a certain theory may seem to account for the whole of certain phenomena, it does not, by any means, follow that it makes us acquainted with the *true* causes of them. The records of science show abundant examples of this fallacy. Neither does it follow that a theory is true because it *seems to be* the only *possible* way of accounting for all the facts. But the spirit-theory, in the present case, does not even account for all the facts; in truth it does not account for any of them, except by assuming, or reasoning in a circle to prove, that spirits are possessed of such physical and psychological qualities as the explanation of the facts demands, which is a wholly gratuitous assumption. But in regard to merely sensuous, visible and palpable phenomena, such, for instance, as the locality, descriptive geography, and habits of the second sphere, which all spirits profess to be acquainted with, how does the spirit-theory account for the wide disagreement and contradictory character of the spirit-evidence? The theory does not account for that, or for innumerable other ridiculous self-contradictions of of the spirits; but its friends are ingenious beyond all parallel at inventing supplementary theories for each particular case, as self-contradictory, however, as the self-contradictions they are intended to explain. But many of them, it must be **confessed, are** extremely interesting for the **perfect** naiveté and innocence with which they are promulgated. Take, for instance, that " cabinet specimen " already quoted in a previous chapter, where we are told that if we adopt the theory that the communicating spirit is scarcely more developed than the Medium, we shall find no difficulty in accounting for contradictions, the ignorance, or lack of development, &c. in the matter communicated. Now, in regard to matters coming under the cognizance of the senses, I cannot help thinking that a majority, even of Mediums, could give a tolerably uniform description of a village in which they had all resided; but, in regard to the other facts to be accounted for, I freely admit that the ingenious author of this sub-theory has hit upon an admirable explanation. So, indeed, the ingenuity manifested in a great many other explanations of spirit-contradictions, if applied to the invention of labor-saving machinery, must certainly bring out a vast number of patentable contrivances. But if the whole mass of the testimony of modern spirits in regard to matters of mere fact—for in regard to doctrine their *opinions* are much more uniform—in regard to such *phenomena* as must come *alike* under the cognizance of the senses or " sense-powers " which *all* the spirits assert they possess—if the *whole* testimony on *such points* were subjected to the ordeal of cross-questioning by a bar of clever lawyers, what would be the inevitable verdict of an intelligent court and jury in regard to the character of the spirits? what, but that of a very competent judge of them in the ancient period, that "*it is their very nature to lie!!*"

There is, however, no occasion to dispute this point with the spiritists; there is no great objection to calling in the gods here, except the ancient dramatic one, " non dignus vindice nodus," the occasion is not worthy of the (" supposed ") company. On the contrary if these people choose to insist that they are the subjects of possession and obsession by spirits from the other world, they ought, by all means, to be indulged in their opinion. It cannot fail to be a stong confirmation of the truth of Christianity for some minds otherwise un-

satisfied—it ought to be for all believers in the spirit-theory—
this proof of its correctness in regard to the so much disputed
doctrine of spirits. Five years ago these same men, who are
among the leaders and abettors of the New Dispensation ridiculed the dæmonology of the New Testament as among the
lowest dregs of "old mythological religions." Now they account for precisely the same manifestatations by exactly the
same theory; only they still eschew "the devil and his angels." *Their* spirits, that foam and rage with the ancient
dæmoniac fierceness, and dash people upon the ground, are
not quite so bad, merely "unprogressed." Indeed it seems
quite likely, from the direction in which they are going, that
in due time they will be convinced of the existence of the other
class—if they are another class—of spirits also, and likewise
of the place "prepared for them."

This matter of the place, by the way, "the bad place,"
seems to be almost as annoying to them as if they were already in it. They lose no opportunity of vituperating, often
with the coarsest and most insulting language, all who believe
that God will make any essential difference, in the future
world, between those who obey him and those who do not.
The most "unprogressed" spirits met with in the spheres
(See Spiritualism, Section xxxix.) are those who have taught
on earth such "gloomy dogmas." who have degraded the
character of the infinitely good—natured, and don't-care-what
you-do-if-you-only-make-yourselves-happy god, by represent-
ing him—oh! vindictive tyranny, and old mythological religion!—as "angry with the wicked." Men ought not to be
made uneasy, and to go along with troubled consciences, even
the short road which leads to whatever kind of everlasting
happiness may suit their taste. On this point there is extant
a vision by the ci-devant Judge (See Shekinah, July 1853,)
which is peculiarly instructive, almost as edifying as the
spirit-confession of the poor hell-fire parson in Section 39.
Their continually repeated calumny, that, to suppose Christ
to have uttered such severe and indignant rebukes of sin, and

threatenings against sinners, as are recorded of him, is a slander against that *good* man;—their everlasting iteration and reiteration of the assertion that hell is only a hobgoblin dream of dead orthodoxy ("so called")—these and many other such-like unequivocal indications make apparent to mere spectators, what perhaps does not come up fully to their own observation, that they have not, after all, succeeded in eradicating from their minds the common consciousness of all mankind in regard to a spiritual retribution hereafter, and—"to compare great things with small"—remind one strongly of the brave boy who was not afraid, but who nevertheless was obliged to whistle louder and louder to keep up his courage. There can hardly be a stronger *external* proof of the truth of Christianity than the constant manifestation, by what the New Testament emphatically calls "the world," of that peculiar bitter hatred of its characteristic doctrines, that vindictive emotion in regard to them, of which fear is an essential element. For such as the Author of Christianity announced would be the relation of "the world" to his doctrines and to his disciples, such has ever been, and will ever be the relation of "the world" to Christianity, from the essential and inherent elements of the character of each. Such, of course is, and will be the relation of the believers in the New Dispensation to Christianity; of "the world" assuming to be spiritual; (while it is only *spirital*) of "flesh and blood" claiming to "inherit the kingdom of God."

Let us, then, admit, since they insist upon it, that they *are* "possessed." The only important question still remains to be decided, what sort of spirits have taken possession of them. Are they good, or are they evil spirits? They themselves admit that they are part evil, at least as evil as any spirits can be, not as bad as the New Testament devils exactly, but evil in such a sense that their communications may be unreliable, and even wilfully false. If, then, any of them are good and true, how are they to be distinguished from the evil and false? There is a very curious peep into the spheres in

"Spiritualism," Section 49, from which it appears that, "very many (spirits) either from an over-anxiety to commune, or from a careless disregard of what they deem a trivial falsehood, assume false names," and we are further told that no one has been more often "falsely personated" than Swedenborg. Was that the case when twenty spirits, voluntarily, "in the Name of God," swore to his identity? Was that the case when not long since, in France, (Cahagnet, The Celestial Telegraph) under adjuration "in the Name of God," which no spirit dares disobey, and after other scientific cautions against false impersonations, he gave responses, on almost all points, *quite contradictory to those he gives here*? Was that the case with the authors of the *profound* ("so called") communications purporting to come from the same Swedish philosopher, and from "my Lord Bacon," in "Spiritualism?" Truly, if any man, who ever read ten lines of Bacon, or one treatise of the thoughtful Swede, can believe that either of those men could have perpetrated, even in their school-boy days, such rhapsodical inanities as are there fathered upon their far-progressed spirits,—certainly, credulity can no farther go, and never was known to go *so* far before.

It cannot be said in this case, in order that "the reader may find no difficulty in extricating his mind from doubts," that it is "an unwarrantable thing to look for instruction much superior to the mental development of the Medium," because in the first place, these were reckoned rather uncommonly wise men while "in the form," and their spirits are now far-progressed; and in the next place, the communications kept clear of the *mind* of the Medium, and only come through his *arm*. There remain, therefore, for all minds not precommitted to credulity, but two possible methods of solution of this difficulty,—the moral and intellectual absurdity involved in the asserted authorship of these communications,—one is to suppose that these spirits were "falsely personated," and the other is to recur to the theory of Synesius already referred to, and to suppose that the brain-dribble of the Medium himself, being in the way there set forth, *expressed*, flowed down through his arm, upon the paper. Incredulous men will adopt some one and some the other of these solutions, for myself, I profess my most religious belief in the latter. How then, provided we could previously know what spirits are competent to make known to us the most important and solemn of all truths, are they to be identified, and distinguished from those who may, under most plausible pretexts, lead us into fatal errors, and delusions? What are the reliable tests? Shall we recur to the ancient and only scientific method that I have heard of, that is, compel the spirit to appear, and judge of his character by the quality of the halo that surrounds him? We are told that spirits can be "identified beyond a doubt," by the test that they are cognizant of certain secrets known only to themselves and the questioner. But do not spirits, according to the highest spirit-authority, and asserted facts, read our thoughts? What need then that they should have known the secret before death? Moreover the spirits read each others thoughts, from which two sources of information, it follows plainly, that any spirit, or at least—excluding the most *material* ones—most spirits can become acquainted with any person's secret whether on earth or in the spheres. This test, therefore, is good for nothing even where it can be applied. But it is not applicable to spirits long dead, and far-progressed, and therefore most competent to teach us—unless perchance there is in the spheres, or somewhere else, as on earth in a less degree, a far-progression in depravity, and development of an intelligent *evil* principle. In which case, what would avail the modern mushroom tests against a haughty and far-unfolded intellect which might choose to amuse itself by mocking and duping men in regard to their most serious relations? Such seems to be the disposition, and the ability too, of some, and for aught that has been shown to the contrary, of all the spirits of the "New Aera," as many Circles in New-York can testify.

Surely there is need of scientific and *infallible* tests, and of the most skilful and experienced of men to use them, in order to deal safely with beings intelligent, it may be, far beyond the measure of human minds, and, for aught we know, as malignant as they are intelligent. But they can be adjured in the Name of God and then they dare not lie! (See Spiritualism.) One would suppose that if they were much afraid of God they would not lie *without* adjuration. But is it not impious, according to the spirits themselves, to represent the good and "impartial" God as *angry* even at the wicked? ("so called.") Why then should the spirits be afraid of *Him*?—this, however, reminds one of another adjuration where the spirits replied, "Jesus I know, and Paul I know, but who are ye?" "The manifestations," as I understand it, are the result of quite recent improvements in spirit-science in the spheres,—how the ancient manifestations were caused the Judge does not inform us,—but the development of the sciential faculties,—to repeat a trite truism—does not necessarily imply any corresponding, or indeed any, improvement of the moral character. This new spirit-science, then, may be used, may have been invented, as well by evil as by good spirits. They may "communicate" as skilfully, exhibit the "physical manifestations" (which though a perfectly natural effect of "progression" are spoken of as equivalent in their influence to miracles,) as remarkably, and, in short, employ the new science in whatever way they please to accomplish evil purposes. The question still recurs, how to distinguish the good from the evil spirits? Oh! but the good spirits teach such beautiful things! Yes, those parks and gardens in the spheres *are very* beautiful! and a god that will never be angry with us—it is very *pitiful* and kind. So we come round to the old principle that the miracle, including the worker of it, must be judged by the doctrine. But, according to Iamblichus, "*an evil dæmon requires that his worshiper should be just, because he assumes the appearance of one belonging to the divine genus; but he is subservient to* (promotes) *what is unjust, because he is depraved."* With what remarkable and apocatastatical exactness this tallies with the experience of certain Circles in New York, where spirits, "falsely personating" the Apostles, preached capital sermons, and yet mocked their dupes with impious, and malignant practical directions. The same opinion, derived like that of Iamblichus, from experience, is also expresssd by believers in the New Dispensation themselves. How, then, *can* we distinguish the good from the evil spirits? or how can it be proved that they are not *all* evil. In regard to all properly spiritual or religious teachings, and teachers, there are but two methods of proving their truth possible or conceivable. The one is the exercise of such plainly supernatural power by the teacher as demonstrates a divine interposition for the purpose of accrediting truths important for man to know; in which case a miracle is as credible as any other effect of a sufficient cause; or secondly, the teachings, the doctrine, must be such as find their full and satisfactory recognition in every human soul, so fast, and so far, as it is *unfolded to a consciousness of its real spiritual character and relations.*— Except upon this condition, *spiritual* teachings, *religious* doctrine, however true, can find no receptivity, or ability to *know* them as true, in those to whom they are addressed. But in order to a *practical* reception of spiritual truth, such a reception, that is, as shall control the conduct, another condition is equally indispensable, namely, that it should find a receptivity in the *will and moral election* of those to whom it is addressed. Hence it is that spiritual truth is a measure and test of the extent to which *the spiritual* is unfolded, and of the character, *as good or evil,* of those who hear it. Hence too, it follows that religious doctrine, that which is truly *religious* and addressed to and testing *the spiritual* in man, must of necessity excite the greatest diversity and contrariety of opinions in regard to itself. Hence, again, the deep meaning and inevitable truth of the words of Christ: "I came not to bring peace but a sword," for spiritual truth, always implying submission to itself, when not loved, is, of necessity, hated. Hence, yet again, the fact that a religious doctrine divides men, who accept it as a religious doctrine, into parties and sects in regard to itself; and, especially, that it is hateful, and annoying to those who reject it—for men rather ridicule than hate a pretender whom they do not fear, — so far from diminishing the probability of its divine origin, is, on the other hand, one of the strong external evidences of its truth. Yet even so, and notwithstanding these and other obvious difficulties of testing the pretensions of a religious teacher by his doctrine, and in spite of the cautions suggested by Iamblichus, and by the experience of others; this second method is still, the true and only reliable one, of distinguishing the good from the evil, the true from the false. It is especially so in the present case, because there is no pretension to miracles here, and if there were, it is acknowledged that the evil spirits as well as the good can perform them.— What then is the doctrine of the spirits and of their interpreters ? And here it is obvious to remark that the doctrine, in order to prove the character of the teacher to be good, must be not only good, not mere sermons from evil spinits, but it must be *all* good, and *wholly* good. What, then, is the character of the most common, prevailing, characteristic, orthodox (about to be "so called,") doctrine of the spirit-theology of the New Dispensation ? And that, not judged by the opinions of a few, or of many, of the present time, which might be to misjudge it; but by the common and recorded religious consciousness of all mankind, to which, indeed, there have been some few exceptions, I dare venture to affirm either from non-development, or mis-development of the spiritual powers. If, then, the devil and all his angels, of the "old mythological religion," in Pandæmoniac conclave assembled, should set themselves to concoct the deadliest scheme within the compass of dæmoniacal craft, against the religious instincts, the spiritual advancement, and the practical piety of mankind, could **they do better for their purpose, than to fill their mouths with** fair words of virtue and brotherhood, and benevolence; for, "*an evil dæmon requires that his worshiper should be just, because he assumes the appearance of one belonging to the divine genus;*" while at the same time, they undermine and eradicate from the soil of humanity all manly virtue, much more all religion, and even all true benevolence, and self-sacrificing love of one's neighbor, which are baseless and evanescent as the morning rainbow portending storms, except so far as they are grounded in the love and fear of God. Could they do better than to make men believe,—if any, even devilish hallucination could make *a man* believe—that they have no *other* responsibilities or accountabilities than those of a tree?—that "moral responsibility" is a phrase signyfying nothing?—that it is impossible for any rational mind to conceive of the existence of "*free will?*"—that *sin* has no existence?—that the universal consciousness of moral guilt and consequent accountability is a delusion?—that all men in the next world will choose their own residence and employments in the midst of sensuous and even sensual paradises?—that God—if he be anything more than the positive pole of the grand, all-productive—for creation there is none—electromagnetic battery of the Universe, or if he has anything to do except to observe the *involuntary* functions of his own body (the Universe) which are the laws of all Nature, man included, who is a part of Nature,—that God, if there be any other God, is too *good*, kind, loving, *pitifully* disposed, even to be displeased at whatever his human children may choose to do; much less, to punish them in any spiritual sense? As for "indignation and wrath, tribulation and anguish," as expressive of the Divine relation to sin, and moral guilt, as far as language can express that relation,—what horrid blasphemy! of the "all-loving Father." Christian reader, do you think I am a man escaped from bedlam, or that I am relating some dreadful nightmare-dream, because such a theology could never have been conceived by any sane human mind? Prithee do not accuse my brain of originating such thoughts even in its dreams. If I found it subject to such, even in that state, I would have inserted in my Prayer Book an extra petition for defence against obsession and dæmonopathy. But that Brains which hail from the second or still higher spheres, are capable of excogitating or adopting, and of inculcating, *for the good of mankind*, such doctrines, I will convince you by quoting chapter and verse from the Canonical Books, and "Divine Revelations," of the "New Dispensation."

And let us proceed in the reverse order, and begin with the character of God; a very important starting point in all other religions with which I am acquainted, but apparently, very little accounted of in this, except negatively: at which I admired, until, in the course of much spirit-reading, which, in some measure, prepared me for something of the sort, I learned that "the soul does not love God objectively, but *subjectively*, i. e. the soul loves God through the centre of its own individuality, and not outside of itself!" (The Present Age & Inner Life, p. 272.) There is no need of an "outside" God! "Deus sum!" I am God myself! the Macrocosm is God, therefore the Microcosm is God! but Man is the Microcosm, therefore Man is God! what occasion, then, to look for Deity "outside" of the centre of one's own individuality?— There are vast numbers numbers of very sincere worshipers of God in this form. This doctrine, however, is not new even apocatastatically. But I also found it authoritatively revealed by an *obsessed* individual, in good and regular standing, that: "Deity (whether "outside" or inside, as I suppose,) is not the legitimate object of man's religion." (The Religion of Manhood, p. 94.) Now this I reckon one of the original thoughts at the announcement of which one wonders that one never thought of it one's self, before. For of what possible use can "man's religion" be to God? Why, obviously, none, the moment one thinks of it. But—I beg pardon of the reader, and of king Solomon; the thought, after all, is but an apocatastatic originality! I had forgotten our Epicurean friends, in whose *religion* also the Divine Nature was:

Ipsa suis pollens opibus, *nihil indiga nostri.*

However, even they held that it was no more than politeness and good manners to offer to the Deity some sort of formal homage, a kind of pepercorn quitrent, although practically, it made no difference to Him, or to them. Even so it cannot to the Deity of, or to the believers in, the religion of the New Dispensation, as we shall see as we proceed with the investigation of the character of the new—apocatastatically new—"outside" Deity. We will begin with very high, if not the very highest authority; that of one who is a resident of the sixth sphere when he is at home, of one who announces himself: "In the Name of God I am Swedenborg." And as spirits cannot lie, "*in the name of God,*" as all the priests and parsons do, there is no danger of his having been "falsely personated" in this instance, and therefore, his teaching must be among the most authoritative expositions of the veritable orthodox doctrine of the New Dispensation. What, then, is the doctrine of *this* Swedenborg, "identified beyond a doubt" in regard to the character of God?

"When the mind attempts to separate the spirit from matter, it has no just conception of spirit. Therefore we cannot invest the Creator with form or personality."——form or personality? do I understand you Sir? do you mean to say that we can not invest the Creator *either* with form *or* personality? or do you mean to imply, as would seem from the context, that form and personality are the same? Is it possible that *you*; "In the name of God Swedenborg," that you, mathematician, theologian, philosopher, metaphysician, of no mean rank in either character while on earth, have *so progressed backwards,* all the way to the sixth sphere, as to have become capable of confounding form with personality, and of supposing that a personal Deity must be inclosed in some human, or other circumscription, and be "located," or move from place to place? In the promised, and I suppose, forthcoming next Volume of Spiritualism, will you have the goodness, my excellent spirit-friend, to explain? The question is a personal one, involving your intellectual character, and I trust for the honor of metaphysics also, and the credit of the philosophy of the spheres, that I have misunderstood you. But let us go on with the quotation :—

"What sort of person would that God be if the form depended upon the idea of man? The form would resemble that of man, as he is supposed to be the image (do you mean in the same *form*?) of the Being who created him. There is no point from which an idea can be formed; (idea of what? of *a form*?) and if with all the various attributes with which the Creator is invested, there is but one point from which any resemblance could be traced, how utterly does the mind fail in carrying out this connection other than through the *whole of God's manifestations of himself through his works!* But the condition of matter necessary for such an *amalgamation* must be unknown to us as well as to you, for if the *identification of spirit with matter* were unfolded to your minds, the *whole mystery of the Great First Cause would be understood.*" (Spiritualism, Section 31.)

Here we have, very distinctly set forth, the identification of God and Nature, or pantheism. The universe is God, and God is the universe. We cannot separate the *amalgamation* here, but we may, in thought, *distinguish* the spirit from the matter of God. How, then, does the spirit act upon the matter?

"When we view Him as a principle, existing in everything, still resolving itself into direct and pertinent manifestation of the incomprehensible specialties of his nature, we have a basis from which we can commence our reasoning." * * * "*In short God exists as a principle.*" (Spiritualism, Section 8.)

That is, we have the "Eternal Laws," which are the Soul of God, and the Matter, which is his visible Body, the Universe. With this doctrine of Swedenborg also agrees the spirit of

Daniel Webster, who says: "The poet was inspired when he said,

'All are but parts of one stupendous whole,
Whose body nature is, and God the soul."
(Spiritualism, Appendix, p. 396.)

I do not certainly know the relative rank and authority of the sacred books of the new theology, or more properly *physiology*, in the ancient sense of that term; but I infer that "Nature's Divine Revelations" is the fountain head of *doctrine*, from the fact that in almost all the spirit-books and spirital literature which I have examined, the essential *dogmata*, and to some extent the language, and forms of expression, are evidently taken from that book. The form and shape of doctrine, there, in regard to God;

"If shape it may be called which shape has none,
Distinguishable in member, joint, or limb;"

is also that of pantheism, the relation of the spirit to the matter, of the soul to the body of the universe being " all variously " represented.

"In the BEGINNING, the univercœlum was one boundless, undefinable, unimaginable ocean of Liquid Fire!" "Matter and Power were existing as a whole, *inseperable.*" "Matter and Motion are co-eternal principles, established by virtue of their own nature; and they were the *Germ*, containing all properties, all essences, all principles, to produce all other forms and spheres that are now known to be existing. The great original *Mass* was a substance containing within itself the embryo of its own perfection. It became pregnated by virtue *of its own laws*, and was controlled, guided, and perfected, by virtue of its own omnipotent Power!" "The Power contained in this great Vortex was the Great Positive Mind!—*and its development was Eternal Motion!* And so Matter and Motion constituted the original condition of all things!" "It was impossible for this internal, invisible, *Positive* Power to exist *without Matter* as *its accompaniment and Vehicle.* In order that this Matter might assume *forms*, the action of the Great Positive Power was necessary to impel it to higher states of progression. So the Matter, thus acted upon, was developed until it became an external *Equilibrium* or *Negative* of the Great *Positive* Power internally acting upon it. And thus Positive and Negative were eternally established in Matter." " The universe must be animated by a Living Spirit, to form as a whole, One Grand Man. That Spirit is the Cause of its present organized form, and is the Disseminator of motion, life, sensation and intelligence, throughout all the ramifications of this one Grand Man. Then, again, this interior Spirit must have a Form, (the difference between the young and the old Swedenborg here is only apparent) through which its attributes may be developed in order that it may be called a perfect Organization ; and *that Form is the expanded Universe.*" (The Principles of Nature, Part ii., or Nature's Divine Revelations.)

Here we have, as before, the Laws of Nature, as the *subjective* Deity or Soul of God, and the visible Universe as the *objective* Deity or Body of God. Or God the inward, objective Nature the outward. Or God the positive Pole, and Matter the negative Pole of this Grand Electro-magnetic Battery the Universe. But is the relation of these two poles of the Great Battery literally physical and without volition as would be naturally inferred from the language ?

" What has saved these living worlds from destruction? It certainly will not be presumed that this is done by a direct exercise of the will of Omnipotence. * * * It would, indeed, be a thankless and laborious work of Omnipotence *to keep his will perpetually on the rack* in order to preserve the revolution and harmony of the planets. * * * The truth is this, *the Deity is himself controlled by the same law* which controls the revolution of the planets. * * * The material universe is the physical body of God. The innumerable suns, planets, satellites, are the vital organs of his body —*the stomachs! livers! hearts! lungs! brains!* &c of his organization. * * * * And the Eternal Mind does not any more *control* the harmonious performance of these legitimate functions of the countless organs of his body, than does man control the circulation of blood. * * * Inasmuch as God is a fact, a Reality, a Principle, it is agreeable with science to suppose that he is Substance—*is Matter*. * * * Inasmuch as God is fixed in Nature, like the main-spring of a watch, or the heart in the human body, so also is his *mode* of existing and acting fixedly determined by the very fact of his being in existence. * * * * He cannot "permit" the great procession of Nature to cease, nor the laws of planetary motion to remain suspended; because these processes and laws are the *involuntary and uncontrollable* physiological, mechanical, chemical, electrical, and magnetical processions of his uncreated constitution. *He did not create these laws and processes—hence he cannot suspend, alter, or control them.* * * * The Laws of Nature, like Nature itself, and the human soul, were not created by the Deity, but were and are, the spontaneous atributes of his divine Existence and constitution. In other words, they are the *inevitable* and indispensable developments of the Divine Essence. * * * The Divine Essence being the *Soul*, the Univercœlum is the *Body*. Moreover, the latter is a *perfect representative*, or in other words, is a bold and clear expression of the interior possessions of the Divine Mind. * * * Therefore, according to scientific principles we are led to the legitimate conclusion, that all the life of plants and animals, and all the phenomena of attraction and gravitation, and of the imponderable elements, are referable to the Active and Moving Principle called God." (The Great Harmonia, iii. 59, and ii. 273, 289, 347, 370.)

We need not inquire in regard to the personality of this God, since the answer can be of no practical consequence. We are told, indeed, that "in one sense he is an individual, and in another sense he is not an individual." But a Being who, or rather which, in all possible relations, acts involuntarily and of necessity, cannot possess the character, attributes, and responsibilities of a Person, in any moral or spiritual sense, or be capable of any spiritual relations. This God is spoken of, indeed as having the attributes of Justice, Love, Mercy, Wisdom, &c., but "Justice is the equilibrium of forces," and so the rest are, and can only be, the involuntary developments, results, functions, of the Divine Organism, more properly *secretions*, elaborated in some of the "hearts!" or "livers!" of *Its* Body. This irreverence, reader, is not mine.

We can understand, now, readily, why it is that "Deity is not the legitimate object of man's religion." Certainly, *this* Deity cannot be the object of any man's religion, since religion implies *spiritual* relations. But can any one conceive of spiritual relations, that is of conscious, or unconscious moral obligations or responsibility to an involuntary law of Nature?—Nature, the external, is a "*perfect* representative" of the internal, or Positive Pole of the Deity. He is *what* He is, and all He *is*, by the "*inevitable* and indispensable developements of his Essence;" so that there is no God "separate from or outside of Nature," or any place left for the exercise of personal, *spiritual*, attributes. However, therefore, men may admire and wonder at some of the manifested functions of this "Animal itself," however the sensational, social, æsthetical, sciential faculties may find their satisfying correlations; the *spiritual* can find none, and Religion is plainly impossible.

"Qua re Religio, pedibus subjecta, vicissim
Obteritur, nos exæquat victoria cœlo."

But though all spiritists and spirits, for the most part, are redolent of "Nature's Divine Revelations," plainly pickled more or less in that menstruum, nevertheless, many believers, still "in the *form*" and "unprogressed" spirits, have not yet risen to the heights of "the Harmonial Philosophy." These evidently are still laboring, to some extent, under the ordinary moral instincts of humanity, or the misteachings of some of the "mythological religions," or, at least, their language often implies, perhaps unconsciously to themselves, that they have not wholly eradicated their hereditary *christian* belief that, "God is a Spirit," that is, a Divine Personality, all of whose attributes are *such*, and exercised in *such modes*, as His Transcendently *Free* Will directs—otherwise He could not be "the object of man's religion," or capable of any moral or spiritual relations. But is this God, in his moral character, in the minds of the even half emancipated (from the errors of Revelation," so called,") spiritists and spirits, the God of Christianity, the God whom Christ "hath declared?" Ah! but Christ has been misrepresented, slandered, that *good* man! he never *did* "declare" any *such* God—the true spirital God is *good* too; what a going back to mythological conceptions to imagine *Him* as capable of being "angry with the wicked!!" Men, indeed, in proportion to their moral purity, in proportion to the true development of the *spiritual* in them, are conscious of very deep feelings of disapprobation, and repulsion, in relation to impiety, vice, crime, wickedness, s*in ;* in some cases, amounting to "an honest indignation ;" as where the impetuous Paul uses that *shocking* expression ; "If any man love not the Lord Jesus Christ, let him be αναθεμα." But this is mere human "*passion*," and "unprogressed" weakness; and to attribute any analogous emotion to God would be to impeach his *goodness! !* and merit the strongest indignation that the *spirital* God is capable of; as witness the unhappy fate of the poor parson in "Spiritualism," Section thirty-nine, who, much to his astonishment, found himself in the spheres, at the very bottom round of the ladder of progression, because, in this world, he misrepresented "a kind and beneficent God *whose only manifestation is smiling on his creatures,* by calling him angry ! !" *This kind* of moral or spiritual relation of God towards sin ; that aspect of severe and stern disapproval and rebuke of moral obliquity, which has sometimes been known to frighten weak, nervous sinners, is very *unspirital* ; it is mere terraqueous humanity "unprogressed." "Nature everywhere is God's acknowledgment of himself, and is enough to satisfy the most earnest longing of all men, if it had not been perverted by the arts of man and the *concerted plans to form a Church on earth* which should shadow to the world *God as a* *spirit*, but in reality, *personating God as a man.*" (Swedenborg, in Spiritualism, Sec. 40.)

If such is the character, and " constitution," of the Deity of the New Dispensation; what, *consequently*, should be the Humanity? The old adage is verified; "like Master, like Man." The God is incapable of moral relations and the Man is equally so. In both, according to the highest authority, there is an *inevitable* development of their Essence under laws which they did not create, and cannot control. Man, not having any " free-will," is not a spiritual being at all. He is an individual, but he can hardly be said to be a *person*, since personality implies " free-will " and moral relations. Animals have not personality, though they may be personified, and the *spirital* Man is only an animal on " a higher plane " of intelligence. But I have promised to give chapter and verse.

" Considering the inseparable connexion which is sustained between the Universe and the Deity, the whole forming one grand System, it is impossible for any rational mind to conceive of such a thing as "*free-will*," or independent volition," * * * * * " Man is a part of this great Body of the Divine mind. He is a gland, or minute organ, which performs specific functions, and receives life and animation from the interior, moving, Divine Principle." * * * * If it can be proved that there are organs in the human form, not dependant on the form for motion, life, or existence, then it may be proved that man is an independent being, and exercises what has been termed " free-will." (Nature's Divine Revelations, pp. 463-4.) " The doctrine of the free-will or agency of the soul, is positively contradicted by everything in nature and man." (The great Harmonia Vol. i i. p. 230.) But what is to be done with the universal consciousness of mankind on this point, which unequivocally asserts moral freedom and consequent responsibility? For the profound logic by which this consciousness is attempted to be proved fallacious, see Nature's Divine Revelations, page 433. There is too much of it for my limits. It is enough for my purpose to refer to it. That such an attempt has been made is sufficiently characteristic of the system which needs it without exhibiting the sophistry itself.— Without moral freedom, there can, of course, be no such thing as sin; for would it not be laughable to hear one speak of his horse as a *sinner*. But, "Man is a part of Nature," in every department of his being, for his spirit is only rarified and attenuated Matter, he is therefore, a part of Nature in the same sense as the horse or the tree. Moreover, this attenuated Matter has been filtered to a pretty high state of purity, for "The innate *divineness* of the spirit of man prohibits the possibility of *spiritual* wickedness or unrighteousness." * * * "Sin, indeed, in the common acceptation of that term does not really exist." The consistency here is beautiful. "Moral death" is a manufactured expression, meaning *nothing*. Spiritual death is only another form of the latter expression; and it never had, and never can have, the least particle of signification." (Nature's Divine Revelations, pp. 413-14, 521.) Now these are what one may call "Divine Revelations," indeed! and cannot fail to afford delightful consolation to "poor sinners," misconsciously such, who find that it was only a sheepish and false humility which led them to suppose that they were worthy of God's displeasure.

In "Spiritualism" the doctrines in regard to the character of man are essentially the same with those just quoted, though less fully, or rather, more guardedly expressed. For, says the spirit-Bacon: (page 209)—"We have felt that the advance of any opinion *opposing the very bais of the faith of much of the Christian world*, would, before the fact of spirit communion being recognized, destroy all that we intended to accomplish." They, (that is, the spirits) therefore, speak more cautiously, and incidentally, yet indicate, plainly enough, the doctrine that *evil* has no *spiritual* origin, but arises out of the imperfection of matter, and other *circumstances*, in which man is placed, or, in other words, man can have no *spiritual* accountability, because he always "*means* well." They speak of "the *evil direction* which *material* connexion produces." (p. 145.) "Circumstances control the acts of man far beyond the belief of a majority of philosophers." * * * * "The good is there, but the evil is consequent on the thousand contingencies which beset man on every side." (pp. 190-2.)

The following throws light in more directions than one. It is the confession of a spirit whose *body*, it seems, had been a murderer not long before, and who, in the language of "the Judge," "came to give his experience, as one who had been relieved from the evils brought upon him by the present ill-organized state of society, and *who, through an evil deed,* (nothing but murder,) *had been ushered into a better and happier state* than that which he occupied while here," "I (the Judge) remarked, *that I supposed it was the force of circumstances* which had led him to commit the deed for which he had suffered?" "That is it, Judge. That is the evil of society." * * * "He said that I must not suppose he was convicted of a bloody crime, and then sent direct to a state of happiness. Oh, no; far from that. But when his spirit was released from his vile body, made so by his evil *passions*, he was led to a spot, and told to choose his companions." * * * "My choice, Judge," he said, "was soon made, for I never loved evil for the sake of evil, but I was *led into it by circumstances*, combined with my unregulated *passions*." (Spirit-confession of Tom Jones Section 27.) The doctrine of the "old mythological religion" that a man is *morally and spiritually, wicked and guilty*, for the very reason that he yields to the force of *circumstances*, and that he obeys, instead of controlling his *passions*, can have no place, obviously, in the New Dispensation, because—the *spiritals* are not in a "state of probation," but in a state of "progression."

Such is the God, and such is the Man, of the religion which, as the spirits inform us, (Spiritualism, p. 227) is to be "universal." So let the stale old mythologies pack their trunks, and prepare to take leave, in search of more fitting disciples; for, "Many globes, spheres, or planets contain inhabitants of far inferior organization to man." (Spiritualism, p. 112.)

The only remaining question of any importance in a religious aspect, whether in relation to this world or the next, regards the destiny of man hereafter. In regard to this world, are men to be restrained by the consideration of any "account to give" after death? and in regard to the next, is there any danger of falling under the severe and permanent displeasure of the Deity? and if so, how is it to be avoided? The answers to these questions follow naturally as any other logical conclusion from the premises already laid down. The case of Tom Jones is a fair specimen of the teachings of the (about to be "universal") doctrine on this point. If a man has been unfortunately wicked—and all men who are wicked, I beg pardon, "*misdirected*," are *unfortunately* so—in this world, from the force of circumstances, and influence of bad company, what does he deserve in the next but to be placed under more favorable circumstances, and in better company? Every man, like the lucky Tom, who was hung in good time, chooses his place of residence and his associates in the spheres.

And as taste is not a matter to be disputed about, all must of course, be equally happy, since all equally have their choice. "The soul is a Cosmopolite amid the eternity of worlds. And is it strange that it should select an abiding place where it can be most happy?" "Well, the soul has waked up in a new body and on a new earth. * * * * * After the natural curiosity of the spirit has been gratified—for under every form of organization the spirit develops its desire to learn—it is chosen, or rather, it selects, by the force and direction of its affinities, the associates with which it will daily mingle, and the neighborhood in which it will reside."— (Spiritualism, 123, & 197.)

True, they sometimes choose very *low* associates, quite vulgar company, and in rather dark places; just as some people select the same sort of companions, and choose to spend their time in the low "hells" of this world, which, however, are quite to their taste—so "unprogressed" are they—and very promotive of their happiness. There is, indeed, one place spoken of,—the witness, being of the celestial aristocracy, had not seen it,—which would seem to have been intended for a place of *punishment*—were it supposable that such a *good* God could have the heart to punish the unfortunate Tom Joneses, and other "unlucky devils,"—rather than adapted to the *taste* of anybody, unless it might be that of a Laplander. This place is described as an immense plain, flat, and without any variety except one mountain. Here the poor spirits farm it. But, miserere mei! *such* a chance of farming! Listen,—"They toil for sustenance, and as their land is *sandy*, and *no sunlight!* (think of that, sinners,) there must be great labor to enable the earth to bring forth enough to sustain them." (Spiritualism, p. 222.)

And surely, one would think so! Try it in the bottoms of your cellars, ye despisers of the sunny spheres, and get yourselves accustomed to it, for thither, perhaps, leads the next stage of *your* "progress,"—unless you can get yourselves hanged and so become deserving of some lionizing and pity. However, these spirits like the place, just as the Dutch like Holland, and as the Vermonters like snow; it is, after all, quite to *their* taste. Because if it is not, they are at liberty to emigrate whenever they choose, and wherever they choose; and from their mountain are to be seen abundance of capital farming lands, with plenty of daylight. Besides, they have a great many missionaries among them, who kindly describe to them the upper country and invite them to "ascend." Hence it is plain that they are very well content where they are. True, "they do not study," notwithstanding that "under every form of organization the spirit develops its desire to learn," "they do not sing," they do not write, but then they have plenty of fighting, (Idem, ibidem.)—the "innate divineness" being "misdirected"—which is as *good* for them, that is, makes them as *happy*, as dancing and whist do the aristocratic spirit-gentry higher up. That is, in short, the doctrine is everywhere fully insisted on in the canonical Books, that every man is to be *happy* in the next world, according to his own standard of happiness.

Rejoice, therefore, and be glad, ye cheaters of the ignorant—ye oppressors of the weak—ye who pervert the cause of the poor—ye unrighteous magistrates—ye bribed judges—ye politicians who would sacrifice the good of your country for all time to some mean and momentary purpose of your own—ye who live in slothful and proud luxury on the bloody sweat of your slaves—ye slavetraders, and dealers, and drivers, and catchers—ye keepers of bloodhounds to hunt slaves withal—ye drunkard makers—ye patent poisoners—ye profane and impious—ye panders to impurity—ye sluggards, idle drones, moths in the hive of industry, lazy wretches, who by the natural laws of "progress" arrive at the gallows, where you accuse "circumstances," and "the organization of society"—ye thieves—ye robbers—ye pirates—ye murderers, assassins, seducers—ye steeped in all nameless vice and crime—ye Burkes—ye Arnolds—ye fiddling Neros—ye Katherines—ye Catalines—ye Douglases—and, *sum of all*, ye *apologists* for all this and these—rejoice, I say, and be glad, at your deliverance from the heavy incubus of conscience which the "old mythological religion" had well nigh fastened upon you—rejoice, for God loves you right well—*do not* suppose that he can be "*angry*," He, "whose only manifestation is smiling on his creatures," and never more so than when he sees them *happy* in their own way—go on, therefore, indulge your tastes; why else were they given you? and in the next world your souls, being "cosmopolites," shall choose their residence, their employments, their company, according to their then spirital tastes and find the next world even as this, only much more abundant.

Christian reader, have I drawn other than a just and legitimate conclusion from the premises? Are *you* ready to accept the conclusion? or to admit the premises? For what are the premises, but the revival of the stale and impudent sophisms which the better heathens, and heathen philosophies rejected with scorn? the same which slunk abashed, for a time, before the polished irony of Plato and the quiet but keen sarcasm of Socrates; the same which insulted the very first Christianity by asserting themselves to be superior to its doctrines; and which confirmed their authority by the same manifestations as now—asserting too, *as now*, that the magicians who produced them were the same *in kind* as the Founder of Christianity, *but superior to him in skill.* (See Eusebius in Hieroclem.)

But sophistry is of perennial growth, and is not likely to die in our time. Are *these* the doctrines which—but I will not insult you by comparing them with Christianity—are they doctrines which—where they have prevailed, as they have often to some extent, and sometimes to great extent—have ever reformed the world, or which would seem calculated to produce that effect? oh, but if God is represented as all love all men will love him!! All men will despise him; and no man ever loved long what he did not respect. A view of the Deity this as degrading to man also as it is to God; for who but an *animal* would desire or accept such a Divinity? What were *He* but a "*King Log*," for filthy frogs first to croak *for*, and then to croak *upon*?

But do not the spiritists and spirits teach morality and the love of one's neighbor? Indeed they do—and for what reason the latter do so perhaps Iamblichus can inform us (see chap. xiv. p. 172)—they do indite of virtue and "brotherhood" as prettily and sentimentally as young misses are accustomed to of friendship. And with such a Deity and Humanity as go along with this part of their doctrine, I doubt not " the old mythological Devil," were he still extant, would agree to furnish missionaries to preach it, (at least spirit-missionaries,) to the whole world; knowing as he must, from repeated experiments, how much the same would be likely to "inure to his benefit." For what is morality eradicated from the *spiritual* nature of man and unprotected by the sanctions of a *spiritual* religion, but a flower plucked from its parent stem, to fade and wither ; or a plant cut off at the root ?

Such is an outline of the celestial, say rather *scelestal* doctrines ; such is the character, in its relations to morality and religion of the movement which calls itself " The New Dispensation," " The New Era," " opportunity not before vouchsafed to mortal man," and by other periphrases asserting its claim to be the result of hitherto unattained " progress ; " and yet, notwithstanding it is particularly—often in the most vulgar and ribald style—abusive of the Bible and all its friends, it is sometimes condescendingly willing to believe that its predecessors may, perhaps, be found among the best of the old Jewish prophets ; and modestly consents to be considered a sort of revised edition of Christianity, its crude, " mythological, " unprogressed," notions of the Deity, of man, of *evil* spirits, of depravity, of sin, and of future retribution, being " *expunged.*"

Does any Christian man, not misnamed such, need more than to know what it is in order to determine his conduct in regard to it ? Certainly he whose feelings do not instinctively repel both its doctrines and its practices, has good ground of suspicion that his name of Christian is only a baptismal one.

Is not, then, so curious a subject to be examined ? Are we to carry our conservatism so far as to condemn all new things unheard ? To oppose all " progress ?" " to cry out blasphemy ? as the Jews did against Christ ?" &c., &c., &c. There are several ways to answer all such stereotype questions " too numerous to mention,"—although I ought not to have forgotten to mention Galileo—which are as convenient for any conceivably, or *inconceivably* audacious scheme of wickedness—take, for instance, as a *second* specimen of the latter, the new pseudo-democratic doctrine of non-intervention, which coolly asserts that if the *stronger* moiety of the *people* chooses to enslave the *weaker* no earthly power ought to interfere to prevent;

which doctrine if democracy endorse it cannot fail to stink in the nostrils of God and Man—as for the most useful science, or purpose of benevolence. That which the moral consciousness of mankind has for two thousand years, condemned as impious, must be excessively impudent to present itself as new, and would not seem likely from its so long and therefore probably, correctly established reputation, to be particularly promotive of true progress ; yet doubtless, could it be approached by the methods of science, and coolly treated exclusively as a matter of science, it is very desirable that science should explain to us *how*, and by what laws of nature or of *art*, of matter or of mind, the phenomena are caused. Let it be acknowledged that the manifestations are not all or even many of them to be attributed to imposture, still it is obvious enough that a very large proportion of them are explainable by the ordinary, if not fully understood laws of physiology and of mind. For if we subtract from the sum total of the manifestations all those which are the effect of sheer jugglery ; all those which are the result of self-deception ; all those which are due to mere " hysterica passio," and other ordinary anomalies, sympathies and diseases of the nervous system ; how much would be left for the spirits to do ? true, if we are to have the spirits we may as well allow them to do the whole if they please ; but if spirits do *so much*, ought they not, logically, *to do more ?* For instance ; being, some of them, extremely benevolent spirits, and highly desirous to emancipate the " universal world " from the thraldom of Christianity and other old mythologies, (See Spiritualism, p. 227.) and to convince us to that end of the reality of spirit-intercourse, and of the real existence of those gardens and parks in the spheres ; being, too, such rapid travelers that they are as good as ubiquitous ; being empowered, moreover, to read one's thoughts, and other sealed packets, much more the daily papers,—why do they not judge, if they are as anxious as they profess, to convince all creation, accept, for example, Greely's offer, and give us by, the hand of Dr. Dexter, the London evening news, to be printed here in the morning—if their locomotives require all night to come over—and put fairly to rout and to silence the cavils of the incredulous. Certainly, if they are what they pretend, they can easily do so much, and beyond all question, if they will do this correctly for one week they will make more converts than the fortieth Volume of Spiritualism will bring over to the new faith in as many years, unless the thirty-nine are to be entirely different from Vol. I. Do not dodge the question, like a Yankee, by asking another; as, why Christianity does not offer similar tests to those it would convince; because such is not the method of Christianity, which offers *spriritual* truths to the spiritual perception and choice of those it addresses, truths which carry their own evidence, and bear their own credentials; whereas, the new dispensation asks no man to believe more than is demonstrated, through his senses, to his understanding. We may therefore, legitimately demand of the spirits all the evidence of that kind which, by their own showing, it is in their power to give, or at least so much as is necessary to convince us. Meanwhile, we are obliged to fall back upon mere vulgar terrestrial science, or even conjecture, to determine whether there are any spirits at all.

Could science demonstrate to the universal satisfaction of men, *how all* the facts are to be explained by psychological or other terrestrial laws of nature, it would be, just now, for many minds, no ordinary boon of science. Or if science could, on the other hand, demonstrate that the spirit-theory is the true explanation, it were better than nothing. Yet when I consider that anciently, for five hundred years, it was investigated by men who made it the study of their lives, men who, in many respects, and perhaps in all respects, notwithstanding the boasts of modern self-complacent ignorance of its superior knowledge, were better qualified for its full and thorough examination than any men of the present time; and who certainly knew how to produce the manifestations to a much greater extent than we; and still find that the result was only the same uncertainty and contrariety of opinions as among us; I cannot help concluding that we have not much to hope for from science.

If science could explain it by the ordinary laws of nature, it would soon die out, with other nine days' wonders, there being nothing, probably, in the terrestrial aspect of it, of sufficient consequence to keep it alive. True, it makes large pretensions in the way of curing diseases, by means of clairovyance and magnetism; yet, I think it cannot be denied that, even without the spirits, it is much more likely to derange the nervous system and general health of those who come under its influence, than to cure those already diseased. For who would choose to subject himself or his children to such effects as are witnessed at biological exhibitions. But if it be admitted that it may in some cases, have proved useful, as almost any other excitement of body or mind often does, it is so manifestly liable to abuses of the worst kind, that there is no occasion to wonder at the ancient dread, and the modern Eastern horror, of the "evil eye." But this is a matter which would, for the most part, soon correct itself—people would learn to keep out of the way of it, or "invoke Nemesis," as of old. It is only in its religious aspect and pretensions that it is of much importance;—if indeed, that can be said to have any *religious* aspect which denies the existence of all *spiritual* relations, and subverts the very ground of all religion. But certainly, only in its relation to that which *is* religion, could it be thought worthy of any very serious notice, much less of the derisive irony, the sarcastic and indignant ridicule, which its boastful and arrogant pretensions, not so much religious, as hostile to all religion, so well deserve, and which, truly is, I think, the only style in which a Christian man can condescend to speak of it in its religious bearings; for who of us would not blush to ask Christianity to permit itself to be seriously compared with such a meagre hashup of heathanism redivivus? But let physical science explain its physical manifestations if it can; let it demonstrate the spirit-origin of its doctrines if it can. It is plain, nevertheless, that the character of its moral phenomena is not to be determined by their origin, or by the nature of the physical manifestations which may accompany them, or by any rules of *physical* science, but by the laws of morality, and the spiritual intuitions of mankind. *Practically*, then, the *origin* of the doctrines of the "new dispensation" is of very little consequence, except that the incautious may be more likely to believe and confide in them if supposed to be of spirit-origin. It is certain, that, taken as a whole, they have had their origin from some *evil* intelligence, *and they are to be judged of and practically regarded in precisely the same way, whether that intelligence is in the terrestrial, or any other sphere.* Let physical science, then, do what it can, or do nothing. We have all the data necessary to determine the *essential* origin of this new (so called) development, its *essential* character, and the science by which to understand and judge it in all its *essential* and important features, facts, and relations. The spiritits cry out "Galileo," and accuse those who do not adopt their opinions of condemning what they have not investigated, and do not understand, and assure us that, if we would attend the "sittings" and "circles," "the manifestations" would not fail to convince us of their origin in spirit-agency; truly! and what if they should so convince us!

Tables move, bells are rung, guitars are played, pencils write without hands, people are slapt in the face, young ladies' combs are thrown upon the floor, their hair is dishevelled, and their dresses and persons otherwise treated in a very indelicate and unspiritual manner, and all this, and more of the same sort, demonstrably, by the agency of invisible spirits; but the same spirits, by various methods, communicate certain opinions in regard to the character of God, the duty of man, and the destiny of the human soul after death;—therefore!! these opinions are true, and reliable, worthy to command the belief, and to guide the conduct of men! "O most learned Judge! a Daniel come to judgement! yea a

Daniel!" is *this* the logic by which you would have us investigate "what we do not understand?" by which you would convince us that the consciousnesses which constitute us men in distinction from animals are mere hallucinations? All religious and moral belief resolves itself ultimately into a matter of choice and moral election, that is, into the degree and *kind* of moral developmeat; "he that is of God heareth God's words;" and these again depend upon a similar choice carrying with it a like spiritual responsibility; he that hateth the light, neither cometh to the light, chooses to remain in darkness.

Let those who choose, or who by the law of affinity are attracted thither, take their place in the animal sphere, emulous of the *instinctive* virtues and of the happiness of the bee-hive and the ant-heap; seeking as the ultimate earthly aim of man, beyond which "Progress" itself can no farther go in this world, the recovery of that "Law of Association" which is his inherently, and which, originally, did actually constitute and crown his unsophisticated high estate, till, in an evil hour, he learned the use of language (see Nature's Divine Revelations) that fatal invention " for the purpose of concealing one's thoughts," and by that learning fell!! "Oh, what a fall was *there*, my countrymen! then, you and I, and all of us, fell down!"

The "New Dispensation," like other epidemic fanaticisms, will have its day. For all spiritual truth, or untruth, I repeat, is tentative, and a test of the spiritual *state*, or character, of those to whom it is addressed—hence false doctrine in religion is called αιρεσις, heresy, or perverse *choice*. And the doctrines of this development cannot fail to find their fitting soil, and appropriate correlation,—in this period especially,—when the "auri sacra fames" has become a wide-spread famine—in the minds of vast numbers of men to whom they are but the expression of their very wishes. Indeed, if we may believe their authors and promulgators, they already meet glad responses from all directions. This is as it should be. It cannot be, and we need not wish it to be otherwise,—for the character is not made worse by the test that reveals it. And in relation to spiritual truth all forms of spiritual falsehood are indifferent. To some, even of these, it may prove useful to find what spirit they are of.

Yet I trust that a large proportion of those who are claimed as believers,—I have myself been reckoned one—are mere investigators of the subject, or persons who are indulging a temporary curiosity, already, to my knowledge, satisfied, in many instances,—that very many others who reckon themselves believers, are persons spiritually *undeveloped* rather than *misdeveloped*, and to whom therefore the error may not be fatal because not wilful—that many others are carried along, or go along, with the movement, without knowing to what they are committing themselves,—their attention having been absorbed by the manifestations without much inquiry in regard to the doctrines which accompany them. To all such, and to all others whose curiosity prompts them to a personal examination of the subject, as say the spiritists, so say I, investigate, investigate, make yourselves fully acquainted with *the doctrine*, and *the whole* doctrine in its relation to religion, and—if you *like* it, if you deliberately *choose* it, I have not another word to say, " non est disputandum," it is not a matter to talk about. *But do not be deceived by the palpable sophism, that, because you cannot account for the phenomena, you are therefore to accept as true doctrines which outrage your religious consciousness.* The phenomena of spiritism (let me repeat) should be divided into two not merely distinct, but different classes. 1st, The physical manifestations—which include not only movements of heavy bodies, apparent violations of the laws of gravity, but the method, the *modus operandi* of all intelligent communications. These let physical and mental science explain—let them *demonstrate* to us—anybody can theorise—the cause or causes of them if they are able ! and if the spirits of dead men are shown to be the agents in the production of the phenomena, be it so, we shall have arrived at the knowledge of *one* fact, a fact, however, *by itself*, of very little consequence. 2d, The moral or religious manifestations, that is, the *doctrine*, or *religious character* of the intelligent communications —and it is plain that the religious character of these communications, so far as they have any religious character, is not demonstrated to be *good*, simply because it may have been demonstrated that spirits are the authors of them,—it is plain that the science which has shown us how, and by what causes the communications are produced may be incompetent to determine the character of them as good or evil. This, in order to be rightly determined, *must be* determined by a different science, but *will be* determined by each individual very much according to his own personal character.

Let then, those who choose and dare, degrade "The Living God" to a "Principle," and themselves to animals, that they may escape the moral accountability of men; certainly *Christians* will not shrink from the high, and—above the whole mere nature-sphere of cause and effect—*super*-natural dignity of humanity because it bring with it correspondingly high and *supernatural* dangers and responsibilities. At the same time, it is not for us to deny that we have forfeited this divinest birthright; to boast of our goodness and self-reliance; or to distrust the consciousness which asserts our guilt, our weakness, and our hopelessness, except through the "*grace*" of a Divine Interposition.

Let those for whom it is the highest conception, fancy to themselves a heaven which shall be as this world beatified, where the senses, the tastes, and the social affections shall find their fullest and most perfect enjoyment; for ourselves, let us be content if we may be found worthy to attain to that world where they "neither marry nor are given in marriage;" where the physiological and sensuous give place to higher relations. Let those who need and dare, invite the presence and influence of familiar spirits, and take counsel of the souls of the dead; for us, it shall suffice, if God take not *His* Holy Spirit from us. Let those to whose character he is correlative, or to whose wishes he corresponds, fancy to themselves, or find in Nature, a God, who in his moral attributes is far below the demands even of the half unfolded religious consciousness of mankind—as if the stream should rise high above its source—a God, who "nec bene promeritis capitur, neque tangitur ira," who cares not for our virtues, and takes no offence at our vices; we will still adhere to Him who is The Holy One, whose definition is also, indeed, *The Good*, but in whose goodness, along with a Divine Compassion unknown to those who have mistaken for it the moral imbecility of their Epicurean Deity, there is inherent and constitutive, transcendent Justice, which, in its relation to *Sin*, is, and can only be "a consuming fire." Let those to whom it is appropriate pay their Nature-worship to the great Productive Principle; their aweless and irreverent homage to the unconscious Immutable Laws; and melt in sentimental emotion at *visible* beauty, or in poetic gratitude to beneficent Nature: as for us, still unto the King Eternal, Invisible, the transcendently personal "I AM," we will not cease to offer, through Christ Jesus, our love and our fear, become one in Adoration.

CHAPTER XV.

"More Last Words."

While the last sheets of the preceding Chapter were going through the Press Mr. Dods' Book, "Spirit Manifestations Examined and Explained," was put into my hands.

Perhaps the explanation may be found in the direction in which he is looking for it. The theory by which he asserts that "the manifestations" are explainable—for it is no more than a theory—is certainly not less credible than that of spirit-agency. It is, however, little more than apocatastatical of similar attempts of the ancients to explain the same things.—Compare what is said on pp. 81-3-4 of Mr. Dods' work with pp. 102-3-4 of the present volume, and page 101, with page 106, also page 185, with page 103. The theories are not perhaps identical—the difference is mostly verbal—but they are about equally explanatory of the facts; yet none of them reach all the *alledged* phenomena. I would that, for the sake of those who are following the lead of the spirits, "in wandering mazes lost," the explanation had been such as could not be evaded by those *unwilling* to accept any explanation but their own. These are the willing, and many of them wilful seducers, without whom few would long continue in a ath which was found to conduct no whither, except to a fools' paradise."

My own plan, as the reader is aware, did not contemplate any investigation of the causes of the phenomena. My purpose was rather to examine the lofty claims of the development to entitle itself "The New Dispensation," "The New Era," "Progress" &c; and its arrogant and impious pretensions to take precedence of Christianity.

It may be thought by some that I have made use of language too severe and harsh towards men who, in my opinion, are merely in *error*, and have only adopted an incorrect theory.

The severity, if such there be, was not intended for mere investigators of the subject, or for those who are puzzled by the phenomena, and know not what to think, or think *wrong*; or for *honest* mediums, or honest believers in them,—except that I do not understand how an honest *christian* can be either a medium for necromancy, or a believer in its responses,—*such* it has been my main purpose to aid, in all love and sincere good-will, in forming *correct* opinions on so important a subject, wherein it is important, that is, in regard to its *moral phenomena*. But if any man can read what I have read of the language of the leaders of the movement, both men and spirits—" Spiritualism " included, notwithstanding what Mr. Dods says of its handsome treatment of Christianity—in regard to God, and man, and the Christian religion, without the feeling of an "honest indignation" which would scorn to express itself as if it found very little to disapprove—truly, such a man is a much better, or a much worse Christian than I am. And tho' an honest man might be in doubt, on looking over the *whole* shallow blasphemy, whether it were proper to think *worse* of the head or of the heart of its authors, certainly he could not think much *better* of the heart than of the head.

Setting aside the religious pretensions of spiritism, it is of no more importance than the feats of Herr Alexander; yet it is probable that nothing less than the most *palpable* showing of *how* each phenomenon of whatever kind has been, and can be, at pleasure, produced, without the agency of spirits, will now silence its claims in that respect among those to whom its doctrines are welcome, and who would gladly appeal to whatever authority may seem to confirm them. And even should full demonstration of the falsehood of the spirit-theory be arrived at, will not the New Dispensation still trust in its clairvoyant seers, and put faith in cataleptic visions, and appeal to its mesmerically evolved divine instincts and intuitions? Though it rejoices in the patronage of the spirits, would it not, without them, and dropping its physical manifestations, still "fit audience find," and that not "few?"

Since, then, its moral phenomena, its religious pretensions, are neither more nor less reliable, whether they are, or are not accredited by spirits, what remains but that its doctrines be judged on their own merits, *wholly irrespective of their origin*, and unprotected by the sophism of their source whether real or pretended; and that men accept or reject them according to their moral affinities, under responsibility to God, and to their own spiritual well-being. So shall it take its place among other infidelities, nibbling at the heel of Christianity, like its thousand and one equally boastful predecessors and allies to be crushed in its turn.

FINIS.

Table of Contents.

CHAPTER I.
THE STARS, - - - - - - - 3.
CHAPTER II.
THE REPUBLICS, - - - - - - 13.
CHAPTER III.
THE GODS, - - - - - - - 25.
CHAPTER IV.
THE COSMOGONIES, - - - - - - 33.
CHAPTER V.
FASCINATION, - - - - - - - 47.
CHAPTER VI.
VATICINATING WATERS, - - - - - 64.
CHAPTER VII.
MANIFESTATIONS, - - - - - - 73.
CHAPTER VIII.
NECROMANCY, - - - - - - - 88.
CHAPTER IX.
THEORETIC, - - - - - - - 99.
CHAPTER X.
DIFFERENCES OF OPINION, - - - - 111.
CHAPTER XI.
ELYSIUM, - - - - - - - 121.
CHAPTER XII.
HEATHENISM REDIVIVUS, - - - - 142.
CHAPTER XIII.
DÆMONOPATHY, - - - - - - 156.
CHAPTER XIV.
DOGMATA, - - - - - - - 165.
CHAPTER XV.
MORE LAST WORDS, - - - - - 200.

Printed in Dunstable, United Kingdom